Presents

Learn Guitar 1
The Method for a New Generation

Written & Method By:
John McCarthy

Adapted By: Jimmy Rutkowski
Supervising Editor: Joe Palombo
Music Transcribing & Engraving: Jimmy Rutkowski
Production Manager: Joe Palombo
Layout, Graphics & Design: Jimmy Rutkowski
Photography: Rodney Dabney & Jimmy Rutkowski
Copy Editor: Cathy McCarthy

Cover Art Direction & Design:
Jimmy Rutkowski

HL14041754
ISBN: 978-1-4584-2471-6
Produced by The Rock House Method®

Table of Contents

Words from the Author

Playing guitar is a rewarding art form that will last you a lifetime. I have spent my career sharing the passion I have for guitar with others. If you follow my guitar method step-by-step you will be successful and enjoy playing guitar for years to come. When I designed The Rock House Method, my mission was to create the most complete, easy and fun way to learn. I accomplished this by developing and systematically arranging a modern method based on the needs and social demands of today's players. I not only tell you where to put your fingers, I show you ways to use what you learn so that you can make music right from the start. I know it is hard to imagine, but even the all-time greats started somewhere, there was a time when they too didn't even know what a chord was. As you progress as a guitar player, keep your mind open to all styles of music. Set-up a practice schedule that you can manage, be consistent, challenge yourself and realize everyone learns at a different rate. Be patient, persistent and remember music is supposed to be fun!

Now, GET EXCITED! YOU are going to play guitar!

John McCarthy

The Rock House Method Learning System

This learning system can be used on your own or guided by a teacher. Be sure to register for your free lesson support at RockHouseSchool.com. Your member number can be found inside the cover of this book.

Lesson Support Site: Once registered, you can use this fully interactive site along with your product to enhance your learning experience, expand your knowledge, link with instructors, and connect with a community of people around the world who are learning to play music using The Rock House Method®.

Quick Start Video: The quick start video is designed to guide you through your first steps! All the basic information you will need to get playing now is demonstrated.

Gear Education Video: Walking into a music store can be an intimidating endeavor for someone starting out. To help you, Rock House has a series of videos to educate you on some of the gear you will encounter as you start your musical journey.

Guitar Care Video: This video will help you with the care and maintenance of your instrument. From changing strings to cleaning your guitar learn many helpful tips.

Quizzes: Each level of the curriculum contains multiple quizzes to gauge your progress. When you see a quiz icon go to the *Lesson Support* site and take the quiz. It will be graded and emailed to you for review.

Audio Examples & Play Along Tracks: Demonstrations of how each lesson should sound and full band backing tracks to play certain lessons over. These audio tracks are available on the accompanying MP3 CD as well as the *Lesson Support* site.

Icon Key

These tell you there is additional information and learning utilities available at RockHouseSchool.com to support that lesson.

Backing Track

CD Track

Backing track icons are placed on lessons where there is an audio demonstration to let you hear what that lesson should sound like or a backing track to play the lesson over. Use these audio tracks to guide you through the lessons. **This is an mp3 CD, it can be played on any computer and all mp3 disc compatible playback devices.**

Metronome

Metronome icons are placed next to the examples that we recommend you practice using a metronome. You can download a free, adjustable metronome on the *Lesson Support* site.

Worksheet

Worksheets are a great tool to help you thoroughly learn and understand music. These worksheets can be downloaded at the *Lesson Support* site.

Tuner

You can download the free online tuner on the *Lesson Support* site to help tune your instrument.

Digital eBook

When you register this product at the lesson support site RockHouseSchool.com, you will receive a digital version of this book. This interactive eBook can be used on all devices that support Adobe PDF. This will allow you to access your book using the latest portable technology any time you want.

Parts of the Guitar

The lessons in this book can be played on either acoustic or electric guitars. Acoustic and electric guitars have the same number of strings and are tuned the same way. Electric guitars need to be plugged into an amplifier to be heard. All guitars are made up of three main sections: the body, the neck and the headstock.

Electric Guitar   Acoustic Guitar

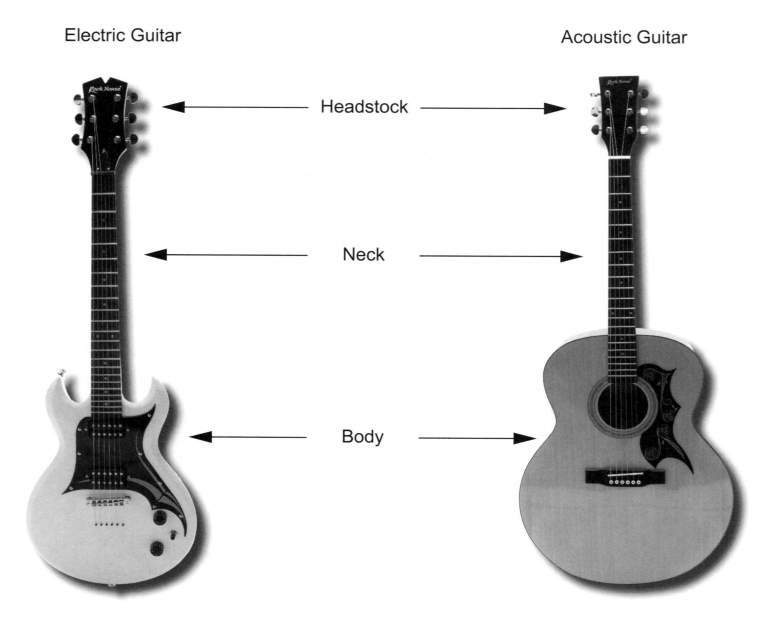

Headstock

Neck

Body

The bridge is the assembly that anchors the strings to the body. Pickups work like little microphones that pick up the sound from the strings. The metal bars that go across the neck are called frets. At the end of the neck is the nut, which guides the strings onto the headstock and keeps them in place. On the headstock, the strings are wound around the tuning posts, and the tuners (also called machine heads) are used to tune the strings.

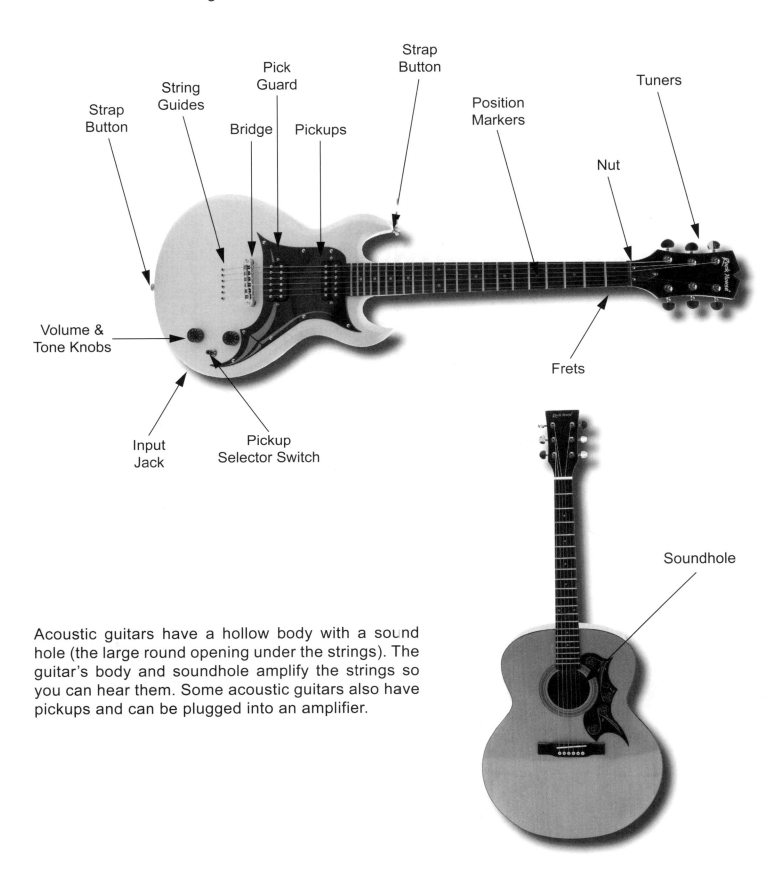

Acoustic guitars have a hollow body with a sound hole (the large round opening under the strings). The guitar's body and soundhole amplify the strings so you can hear them. Some acoustic guitars also have pickups and can be plugged into an amplifier.

Holding the Guitar & Pick

Throughout this book, we will refer to the picking hand as your right hand, and the fretting hand as your left hand, left handed players take note. While sitting or standing always angle the guitar neck up at a 30 degree angle. Find a comfortable chair with no arms where your feet are flat on the floor.

Holding the Guitar

Right Hand Position

Place your right hand forearm on the top of the guitar body. Drape your arm and hand over the strings almost parallel with the bridge. Anchor one or more of your fingers onto the guitar body. This will help gauge your pick placement.

Left Hand Position

Hold your left hand in front of the neck, wrist straight and curl your fingers in to make a "C" shape with your hand. Bring your hand to the neck in a comfortable and natural fashion. Be sure to place your thumb in the middle of the back of the neck. If your wrist is bent raise the guitar neck higher until it is straight.

Holding the Pick

Center the pick on the index finger of your right hand. Bring your thumb down on top of the pick. Pinch your thumb and finger together and leave just the tip of the pick showing. Leave your hand open and your other fingers relaxed (don't make a fist).

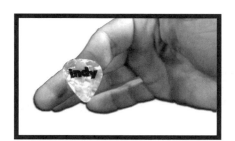 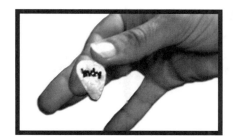 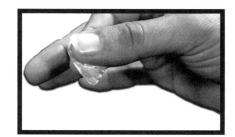

Names of the Open Strings & Tuning

CD Track 2

The fattest string is the 6th string and the thinnest is the 1st string. A great way to remember the open strings is to use an acronym creating a word for each letter name. The following is a silly acronym I created: Every – Bad – Girl – Deserves – Another – Egg. Make up you own saying for the open strings.

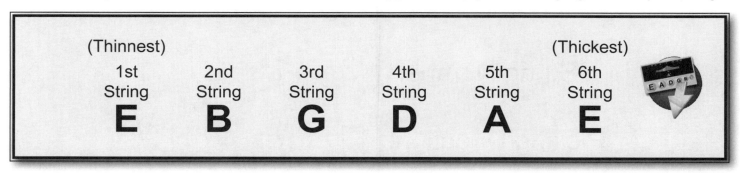

(Thinnest)				(Thickest)	
1st String	2nd String	3rd String	4th String	5th String	6th String
E	B	G	D	A	E

Tuning

Tune your guitar using the machine heads on the headstock. Tighten the string to raise the pitch. Loosen the string to lower the pitch. Be careful not to accidentally break a string by tightening it too much or too quickly. The easiest way to tune a guitar is to use an electronic tuner. You can download your free online tuner from RockHouseSchool.com.

Open String Picking Pattern

CD Track
3

Picking Symbols

There are two different ways to pick a string: down or up. The symbols below are used to indicate a down pick or an up pick. Practice picking down and up on the 6th string for a few minutes.

⊓ = Down Pick (Toward the Floor)

V = Up Pick (Toward the Ceiling)

An easy way of remembering which symbol is which in the beginning, is to realize that the open side of each symbol is in the direction of the pick stroke that it represents.

Pick each open string individually in the order shown. To get even, steady picking use alternate picking, this is a down-up-down-up picking motion. Repeat the pattern for two minutes without stopping. As you progress keep adding more time.

String Number: 3   1   2   1

Picking Direction: ⊓   V   ⊓   V

Finger Numbers

As you progress through this book I will be referencing your fretting hand fingers with numbers. Memorize these now so you can follow along with ease.

Left hand or fretting hand:

Index Finger = 1

Middle Finger = 2

Ring Finger = 3

Pinky Finger = 4

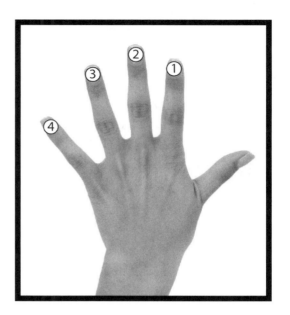

Reading Chord Charts

A chord is a group of notes played together. A chord chart (chord diagram) is a graphic representation of part of the fretboard (as if you stood the guitar up from floor to ceiling and looked directly at the front of the neck). The black dots within the graph represent fretted notes and show you where your fingers should go, the number within the black dots represent the proper finger to use.

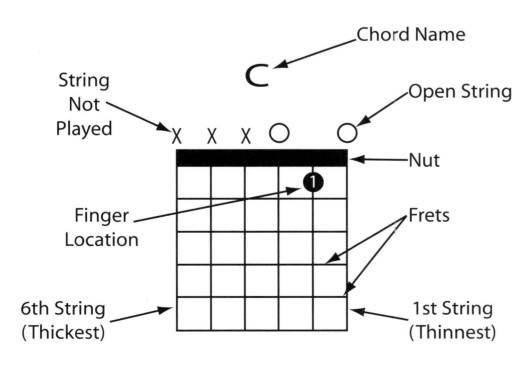

For each finger location dot you need to find three things that will tell you where each note will be played:

> 1. The Finger
> 2. The Fret
> 3. The String

Your First Chords

CHORD PROFESSOR

Keep your thumb anchored against the back of the neck. Press down the notes with your fingertips just to the left of (behind) the fret pressing the string inward toward the neck and make sure to arch your fingers so they don't touch the other strings. The lowest three strings in each chord have an "X" above them and are not played. Pick the notes of each chord, one at a time. Once you can sound all the notes strum each chord by striking all three notes downward together in one comfortable strumming motion.

Remember for each finger location dot find:
1. The Finger   2. The Fret   3. The String

C

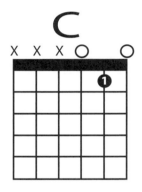

G

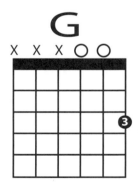

E

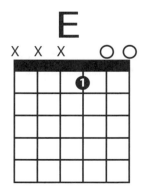

Chord Picking Pattern

While fretting the G and C chords pick out the notes individually using the 3 – 1 – 2 – 1 picking pattern. Follow the repeat signs and play the pattern twice for each chord. Be sure you're using alternate picking. Start out slowly and build your speed gradually.

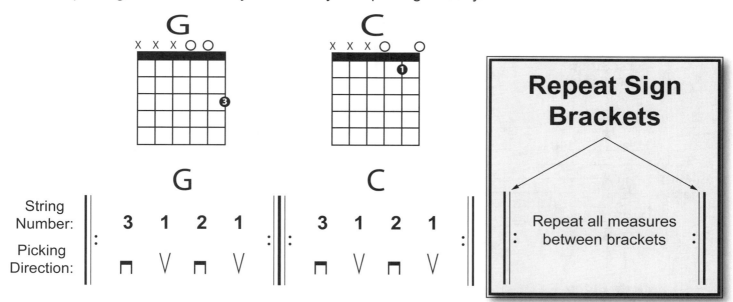

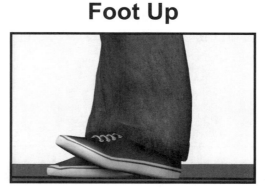

Repeat Sign Brackets

Repeat all measures between brackets

Counting Beats

A beat is the basic unit of time in music. A common way to count beats is to tap your foot. One beat would equal tapping your foot down-up. Tap your foot and count 1 – 2 – 3 – 4 repetitively, say each number as your foot hits the ground. You will learn different note types that tell you how many beats to let notes ring.

Foot Down   **Foot Up**

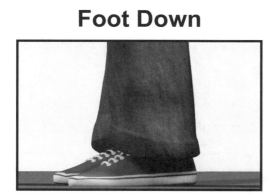

The Metronome

A metronome is a device that clicks at an adjustable rate you set. It will help you develop a sense of timing and gauge your progress. By playing along with the clicking sound you get the sense of playing with another musician. Each click represents one beat. I will note the best times to use a metronome throughout this program with a metronome icon. If you don't have a metronome you can download one from the *Lesson Support* website.

Reading Tablature

Tablature (or tab) is a number system for reading notes on the guitar. The six lines of the tablature staff represent each of the strings on the guitar. The top line is the thinnest (highest pitched) string. The numbers placed directly on these lines are the fret number to play each note. Underneath the staff, is a series of numbers that tell you which left hand finger to fret the notes with. The tablature staff is divided into a small sections called measures by bar lines.

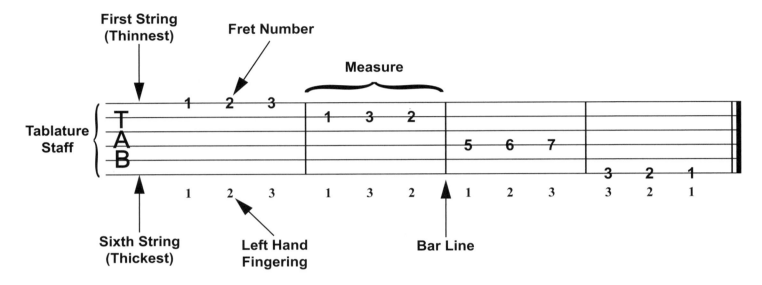

Tablature Riffs

CD Track
6

A riff is a short rhythmic phrase. Riffs are found in many songs and are often the main hook of a song. The following are two riffs written in tablature. These are simple, fun riffs that will give you your first experience reading tablature. Learn each example separately then put them together and play them in a row.

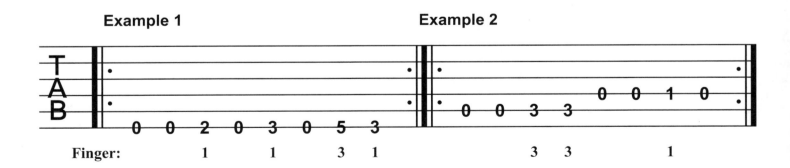

Timing Explanations - Note Values

The Parts of a Note

The HEAD

The STEM

The FLAG

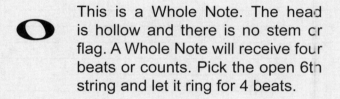

The Types of Notes

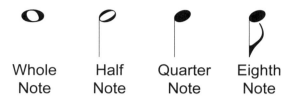

Whole Note   Half Note   Quarter Note   Eighth Note

Whole Notes = 4 Beats

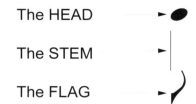 This is a Whole Note. The head is hollow and there is no stem or flag. A Whole Note will receive four beats or counts. Pick the open 6th string and let it ring for 4 beats.

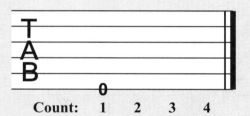

Count: 1   2   3   4

Half Notes = 2 Beats

 This is a Half Note. The head is hollow and there is a stem. A Half Note will receive two beats or counts. Pick the open 6th string on beats 1 and 3.

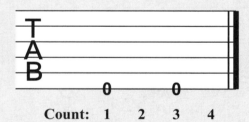

Count: 1   2   3   4

Quarter Notes = 1 Beat

 This is a Quarter Note. The head is solid and there is a stem. A Quarter Note will receive one beat or count. Pick the 6th string on every beat.

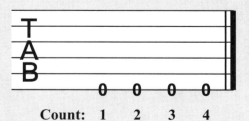

Count: 1   2   3   4

Notation in Tab

Throughout this book you will see that many of the tablature staffs have rhythms written with the notes. Here is what the rhythmic notations look like on the tab staff.

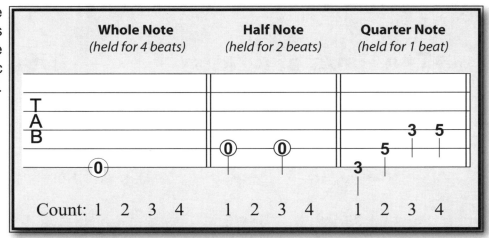

Whole Notes

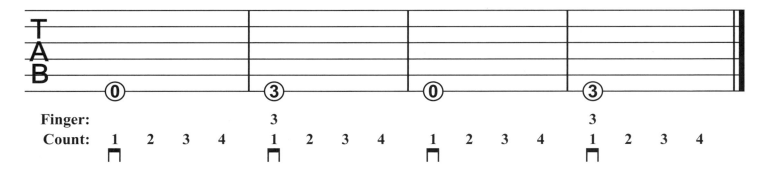

Half Notes

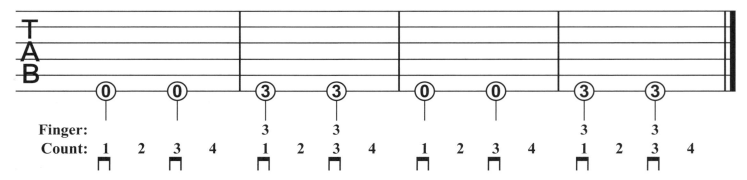

Quarter Notes

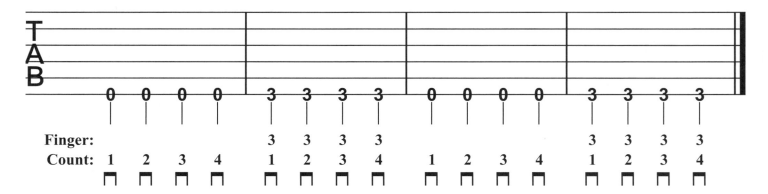

Time Signatures

Time signatures are written at the beginning of a piece of music. The sole function of a time signature is to tell you how to count the music. The top number tells you how many beats there are in each measure and the bottom number tells what type of note receives one beat. Time signatures will be used where specific timing is indicated in this book.

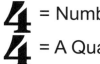 = Number of beats per measure.

= A Quarter note receiving one beat.

Indicates four beats per measure.

Indicates three beats per measure.

Single Note Melodies

Aura Lee

CD Track

8

This is your first single note melody. You will be using quarter and half notes to play this melody. Pay close attention to the fingering and count below the staff.

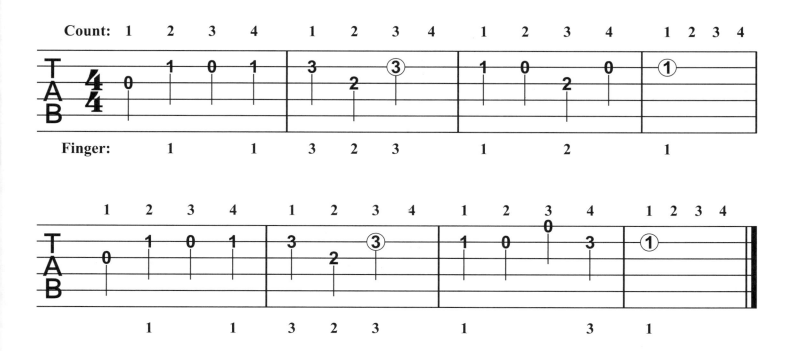

Rockin' the Bells

In this melody you will be playing quarter, half and whole notes. Practice each line separately then put the whole song together. Once you can play the song from beginning to end without stopping, play it along with the full band backing track.

Teacher Accompaniment:

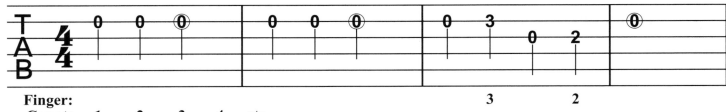

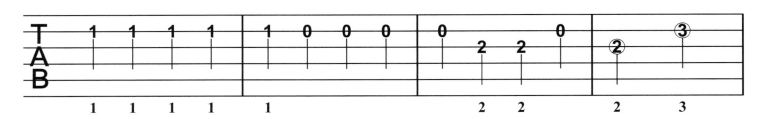

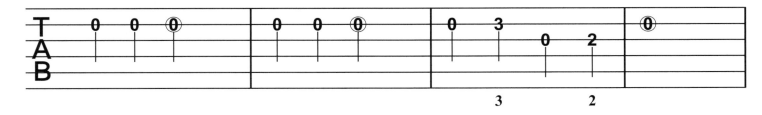

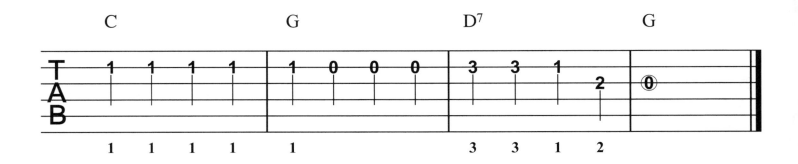

18

Rhythm Notation

Songs are created when you combine chords together to form progressions. Rhythm notation will be used in this book to show you how to strum each chord. The note values you learned will indicate the rhythm to strum each chord. The basic appearance of each note type will be the same but with a slightly different shape.

Whole Note   **Half Note**   **Quarter Note**

The following is an example of a rhythm chord progression. The chord names are written above the staff, and the rhythm notation indicates the rhythm in which the chords are strummed.

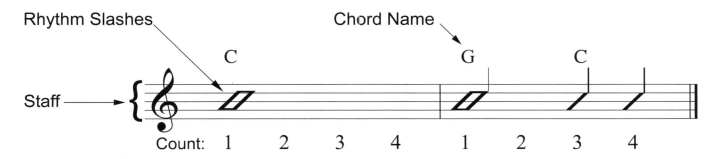

Counting with a Drum Beat

CD Track 11

To better understand timing let's count along with a drum beat. The drum backing track for this lesson has a snare and bass drum played in 4/4 timing. As the drum beat is playing count 1 - 2 - 3 - 4 and repeat this count. The 1 and 3 are counted when you hear the bass drum which is the big bass toned drum; while 2 and 4 are counted on the snare drum which is the higher pitched drum that has a bit of rattle to its sound. The next step is to get your "body clock" into the mix. Your body clock is basically moving your body to the music. One of the simplest ways to do this is by tapping your foot. Every count should be when your foot hits the ground, like you are stepping on it.

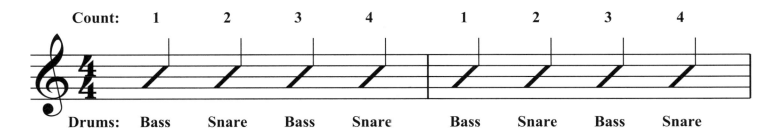

After you feel comfortable counting and tapping along with the backing track, count and tap along with your favorite songs or music on the radio. Listen for the bass and snare drum, these two drums are the backbone of a song's rhythm.

Strumming Chords

Now take the G and C chords and play them in a rhythm chord progression. There are three variations using whole, half and quarter note strumming. Strum the chords by pivoting from your elbow to rake the pick across the strings in one swift motion. Use all down strums and keep your arm relaxed. Playing these rhythms over the bass and drum backing track will give you the feel of how it is to play with a full band.

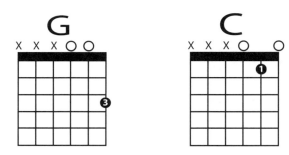

Whole Notes

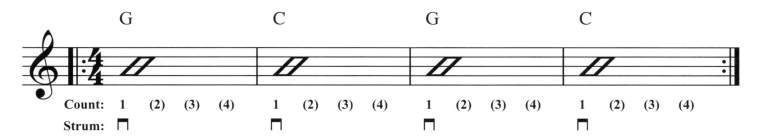

Below is the same rhythm with half and quarter note strumming. For half notes you will strum each chord two times per measure. For quarter notes strum each chord four times for each measure. Every time your foot hits the ground you strum. Make sure to play these rhythms over the bass and drum backing track, this will let you feel how it is to play with a full band.

Half Notes

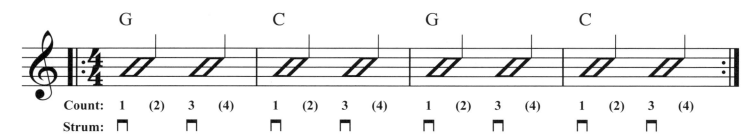

Quarter Notes

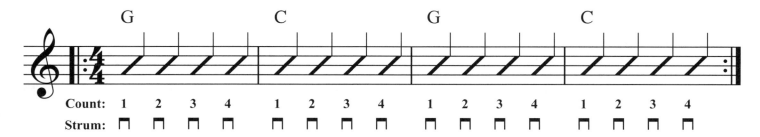

Minor Chords

CHORD PROFESSOR

Minor chords have a sad sound while major chords have a happy sound. Minor chords are presented in this book with a capital letter, which refers to the letter name of the chord, followed by a lowercase "m" indicating that it is a minor chord. Remember to keep your thumb firmly anchored against the back of the neck.

Am

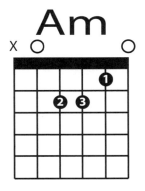

Em

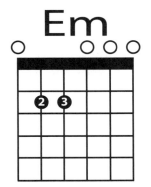

Major & Minor Sounds

You will learn major and minor chords in this book. Major chords have a happy or bright sound. Minor chords have a sad or melancholy sound. If someone was writing a song about the happiest day of their life they would use major chords. But if they were writing a song about a friend moving away they would surely use minor chords.

Chord Progression

Now let's put the minor chords into a chord progression. Strum each chord down two times using half note timing. You will strum on the 1 and 3 beats of each measure. The backing track will have drums and bass guitar, play along with this track and get the sensation of playing in your own band.

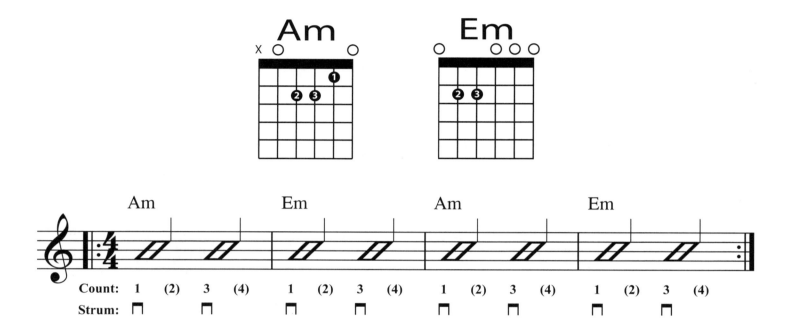

MUSIC ASSIGNMENT

Now take these two chords and change the timing to quarter note strumming. Strum each chord down four times. You can use the same bass drum backing track to play this variation over.

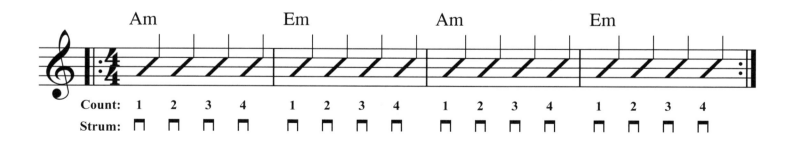

Learn Guitar 1 - Quiz 1
Once you complete this section go to RockHouseSchool.com and take the quiz to track your progress. You will receive an email with your results and suggestions.

Attaching Your Strap

To stand up and play you must attach a strap to your guitar. Most electric and acoustic guitars have strap buttons on both sides of the guitar body to attach the strap. Some acoustic guitars don't have a strap button on the neck side of the body. Attach the strap with a string tying it around the neck after the nut of the guitar on the headstock. Don't adjust the strap too low and keep a consistent guitar position sitting and standing. You should always have the neck of your guitar pointed up at about a 30 degree angle to ensure proper hand position.

 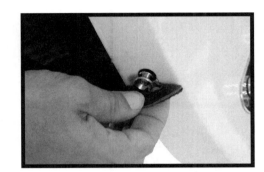 

CD Track
21

Single Note Riffs

Pay close attention to the finger used to play each note. Start at a slow steady tempo and build speed gradually.

Example 1

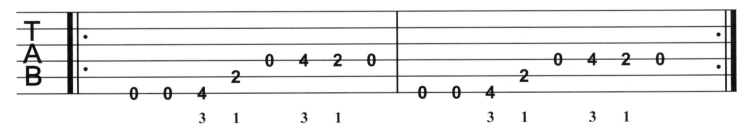

Example 2

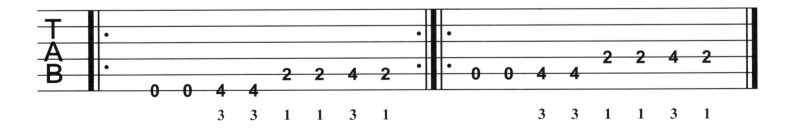

Major Chords

CHORD PROFESSOR

The following open major chords are commonly used in songs. On the A chord diagram, the slur (curved line) going across the top of the diagram indicates you should bar those notes. A bar is executed by placing one finger flat across more than one string. Pick each note of these chords individually to make sure you're applying enough pressure with your fingers, and then strum all the notes together.

A

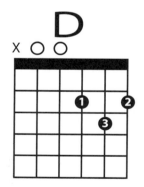

D

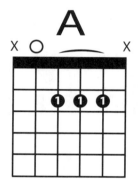

E

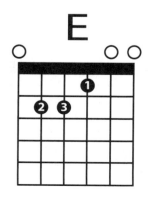

Eighth Notes

An eighth note receives ½ beat of sound and divides a quarter note in half. For every one beat you will play two notes. You will also use a different count. Instead of 1 - 2 - 3 - 4, sub-divide that in half and count 1 & 2 & 3 & 4 &. The 1, 2, 3 and 4 are when your foot hits the ground; each "&" is when your foot goes up in the air.

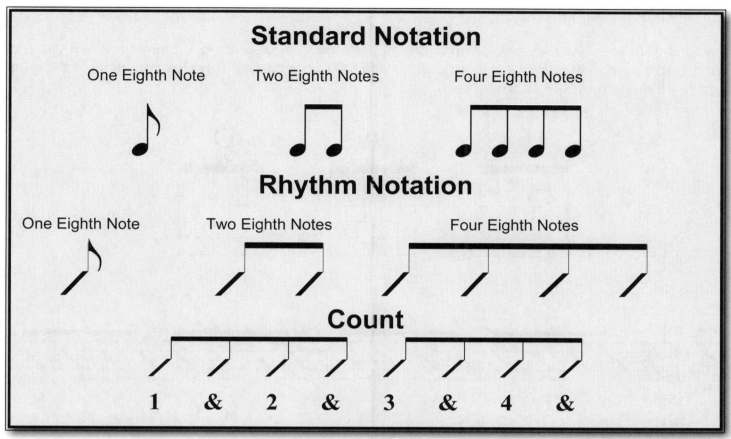

Here is an exercise playing eighth notes. While picking your 6th string open tap your foot and play it in eighth notes. Use alternate picking while playing this to gain speed and fluidity.

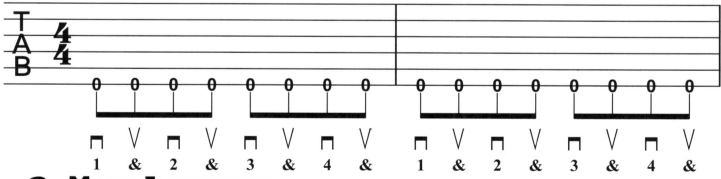

MUSIC ASSIGNMENT

Play eighth notes along with the drum beat from the "Counting Along with a Drum Beat" lesson. Pick eighth notes starting on the low E string and then down all six strings. Tap your foot and use alternate picking; your foot and pick should go down and up in sync.

Song Progression

The strum pattern for this progression is alternate strummed eighth notes. Strum each chord eight times using a down - up alternate strum pattern. When alternate strumming keep your hand, arm and shoulder relaxed and loose. Pivot the strum from your elbow moving the pick across the strings in a down up motion. Don't strum too far up or down past the strings, keeping a small range of motion. Grip the pick loosely to avoid a stiff sound.

Remember to keep your shoulder, arm and hand loose and relaxed when strumming. When you feel comfortable playing the progression try it along with the backing track. Pay close attention to the bass and snare drum to keep your timing even.

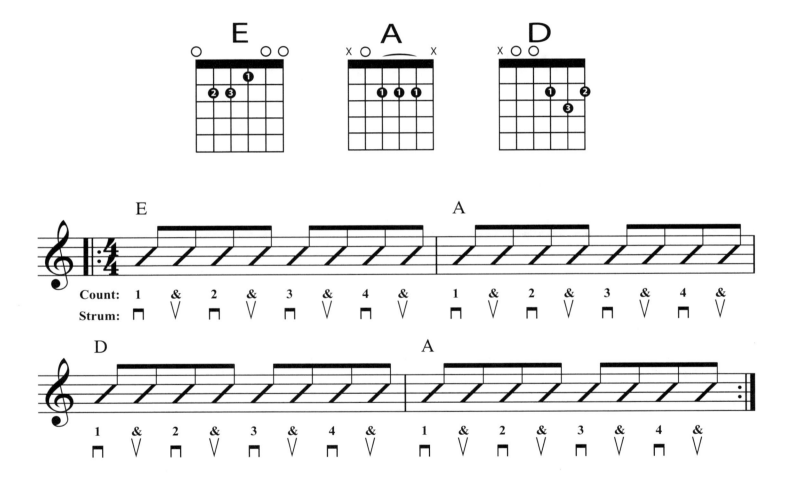

MUSIC ASSIGNMENT

Count along with your strumming 1 & 2 & 3 & 4 & for each chord. This will help you feel the timing and get more familiar with the most common time signature 4/4 timing. Once you feel comfortable counting, tap your foot along with your strumming to get your body clock in motion.

26

Picking Exercise

This picking sequence will challenge your pick and help build coordination. Use consistent alternate picking and build your speed up gradually. Pick the open strings in succession in the following order 4-1-3-1-2-1. The 1st string will always be played with an up pick. You should play this with a metronome to gauge your progress increasing your speed gradually each day. After you have this pattern memorized, use this same pattern with all the chords you have learned so far. Fret the chord and pick the 4-1-3-1-2-1 pattern.

Quick Tip: Try not to look at your picking hand when doing this exercise. You need to train your hand to sense where the strings are instinctively.

String Pattern: 4 - 1 - 3 - 1 - 2 - 1

67 bpm

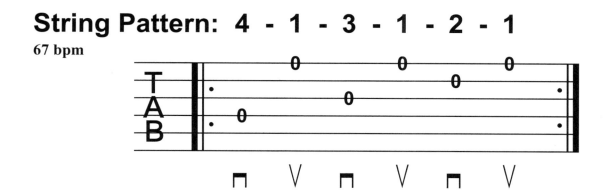

Chord Picking Pattern #2

Chord progressions can be played using strumming or picking techniques. Here is a picking pattern applied to the E and A minor chords. The picking pattern for E minor is 6-5-4-3-2-3-4-5; and the pattern for A minor is 5-4-3-2-1-2-3-4. Make sure to use alternate picking. After you have this pattern mastered, play it with the backing track.

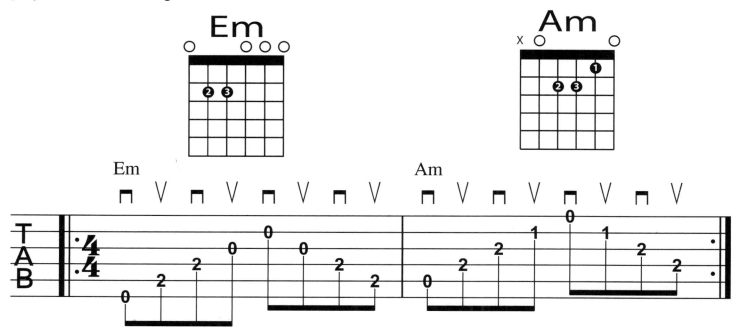

Chords in Tablature

Chords can also be written in tablature. If there are several numbers stacked together in a column, those notes should be played (or strummed) at the same time. Here are a few examples of chords written in tablature:

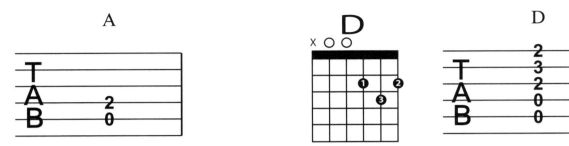

CD Track

29-30

Blues in A

Blues has influenced almost every genre of music. A basic understanding of the blues will give you a great advantage as a guitarist. The following blues progression is a series of two note chords. Each has an open string as the lower pitched note. This is a 12 bar blues progression which means it consists of 12 measures. This progression should sound familiar; it's the foundation for many rock and blues songs. First, play through the progression with a straight feel (an even, steady pattern).

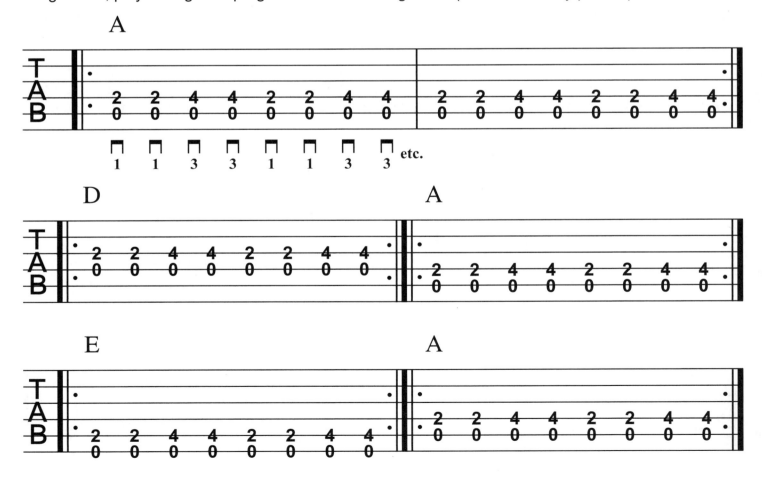

The Shuffle Feel

The shuffle feel is a common rhythm that has been used by many great blues artists. This uneven rhythm, also called the swing feel, has a bouncy feel that makes your body sway to the music. Play the example below of the shuffle feel. The way the notes are spaced depicts the timing.

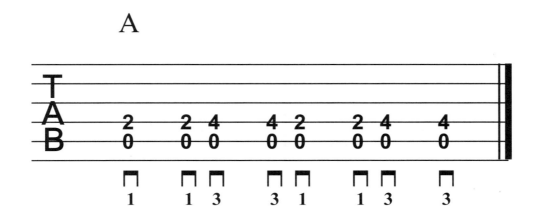

Now play the blues in A rhythm with the shuffle feel. Once you can play the progression with this feel, play it with the backing track.

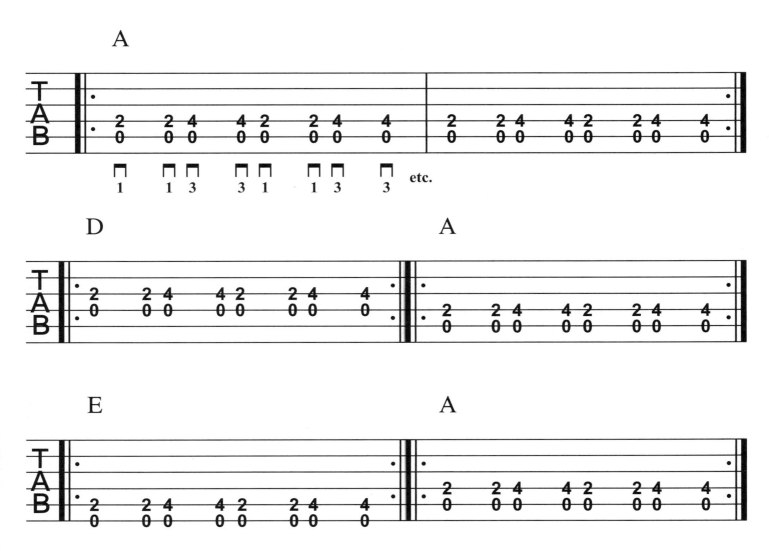

Eighth Note Riffs

These two riffs are in steady eighth note timing. Count along as you play to feel the rhythm. Use alternate picking as you play each riff.

Example 1

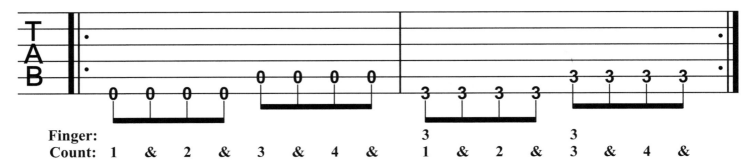

Example 2

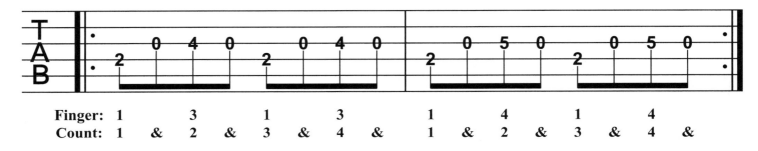

Rests

W

The next melody contains your first rests. A rest is a period of silence. Like whole, half and quarter notes you keep time only there is no sound. See what each rest looks like below.

Whole Rest 4 Beats	Half Rest 2 Beats	Quarter Rest 1 Beat	Eighth Rest 1/2 Beat

| count: | 1 2 3 4 | 1 2 3 4 | 1 2 3 4 | 1 & 2 & 3 & 4 & |

When the Saints Go Marching In

Here is another single note melody. Pay close attention to the rests within the song and stop the strings from ringing for the time duration of each. A tie is a curved line that connects two or more of the same notes together. You pick the first note and let it ring for the duration of both. There is a tie in the last two measures of this song.

Teacher Accompaniment:
95 bpm

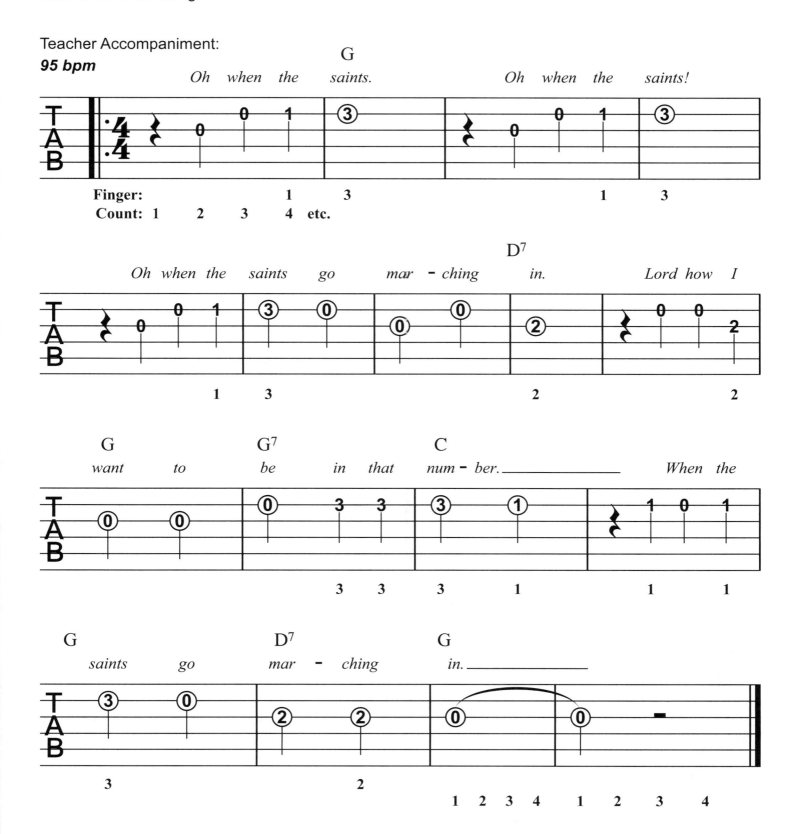

The Chromatic Scale

Intervals – The Half Step

An interval is the distance between two notes. Intervals come in different sizes gauged by the distance between the notes. If the notes are sounded in a row, it is a melodic interval. If sounded together, it is a harmonic interval. The smallest interval in music is the half step. A half step would be the distance of one fret on the guitar. If you play any note and then play the note at the next fret you are playing a half step. A whole step is made up of two half steps.

Sharps and Flats

A sharp "#" means higher in pitch by a half step or one fret. A flat "b" means lower in pitch by a half step or one fret. Sharps and flats are used in music when creating chords and scales and are also referred to as accidentals.

$$\flat = \text{Flat} \qquad\qquad \sharp = \text{Sharp}$$

The Chromatic Scale

All the music we listen to is derived from a group of 12 notes known as the Chromatic Scale. It doesn't matter if it's a complicated classical piece or a simple punk rock song, they are all composed using these 12 notes. These 12 notes are all a half step apart. There are two natural half steps in music: B to C, and E to F. There will not be a sharp between these notes. Study and memorize the Chromatic Scale below because we will reference and apply it to the guitar throughout this book:

Natural Half Steps

A   A#/Bb   B   C   C#/Db   D   D#/Eb   E   F   F#/Gb   G   G#/Ab   A

Notice that there is a common flat and sharp note, one note with two different names such as A#/Bb. This is because if you start with an A note and raise it a half step it would be called A#. If you start with a B note and lower it a half step it would be called Bb. Same note, different name. These are called enharmonic notes.

MUSIC ASSIGNMENT

Write out the chromatic scale on a piece of paper starting from A and going back to A. Be sure to put the enharmonic sharps and flats on the paper. Next, if you feel courageous, try writing it backwards from A to A. The better you have this memorized, the easier you will be able to follow this book.

Notes in the First Position

It's important to learn the names of the notes on your guitar so you can communicate with other musicians effectively. The first position is considered the first four frets of the guitar. Using the names of the open strings and the chromatic scale you can learn the notes on the first position of your guitar.

Let's outline the names of the notes on the first position of the guitar. Start with the sixth string open E and go up the chromatic scale from there: F first fret, F# second fret, G third fret, G# fourth fret. Next, do this same process on the other five strings. Even though you can see the notes written out below, it is important to practice each string without looking and memorize the note names.

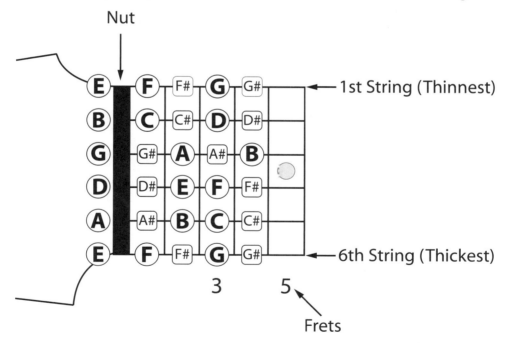

Here is what the notes in the first position look like when written on a neck diagram:

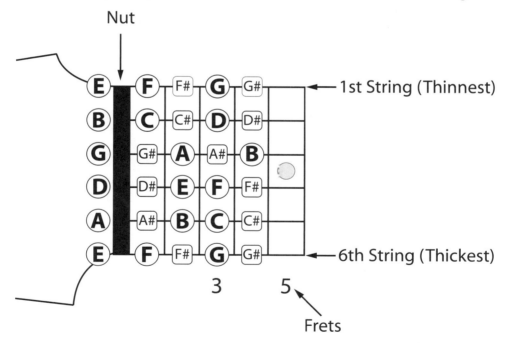

Blues Riff Rhythm

The following is a single note blues riff rhythm. There are many times in music where a rhythm for a song will be constructed using single notes instead of chords. This is a common rhythm so it should sound familiar. Be sure to play this over the bass and drum backing track.

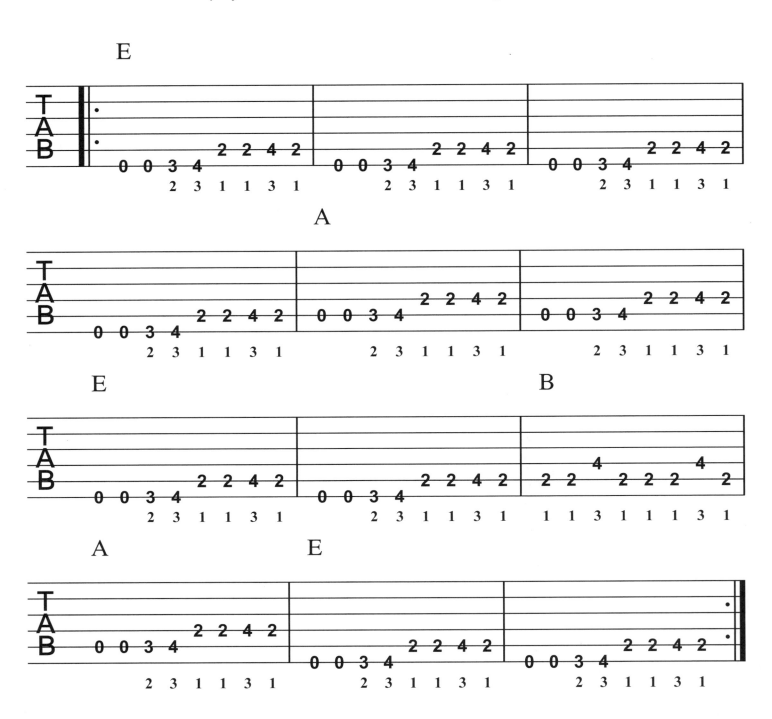

MUSIC ASSIGNMENT

This rhythm can be played with the shuffle feel that you learned in the Blues in A lesson. Below are the first few measures with the shuffle feel rhythm to get you started:

E

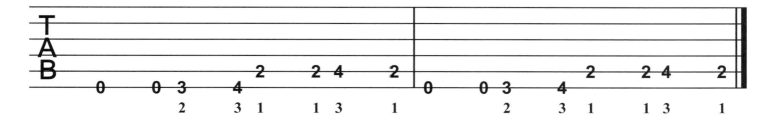

CD Track
39

Single Note Riffs #2

The following riffs have rhythms that are uneven. The spacing of the notes will depict the timing rhythm. The curved line in Example 2 is above three notes that should be picked quickly with alternate picking.

Example 1

The Mission

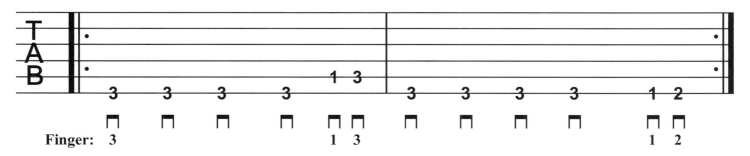

Example 2

Bonded

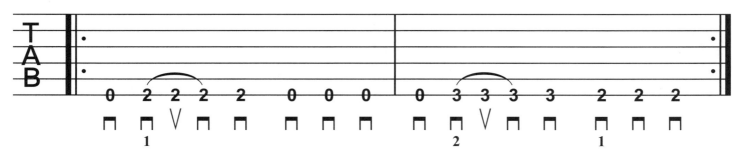

How to Read a Scale Diagram

Scale diagrams are simply a diagram outlining where the notes of a scale are located on the guitar neck. The six lines that go from left to right represent each of the six strings. Like with tablature, the top line is the thinnest (highest pitched) string and the bottom line is the thickest (lowest pitched) string. The lines running from top to bottom are the frets. The numbered dots placed directly on a string show you the specific fret to play each note, and the number inside indicates which left hand finger to fret the note with. The numbers underneath the diagram indicate where on the neck the scale is located, in this diagram the scale begins at the 5th fret:

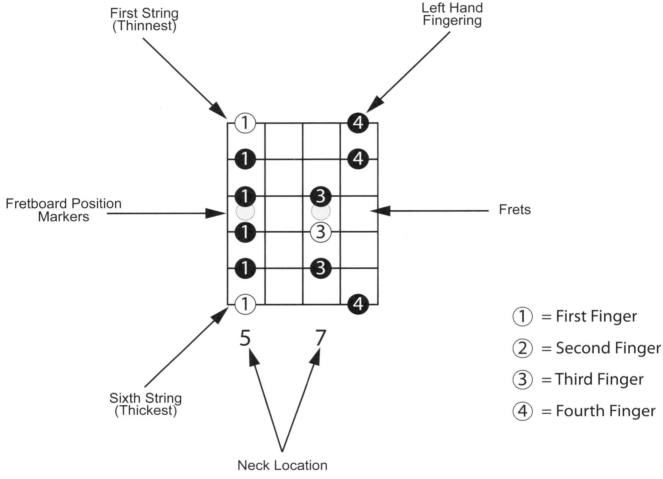

Notice how the diagram above is a mirror image of the guitar neck. Below see how this scale pattern looks on the guitar.

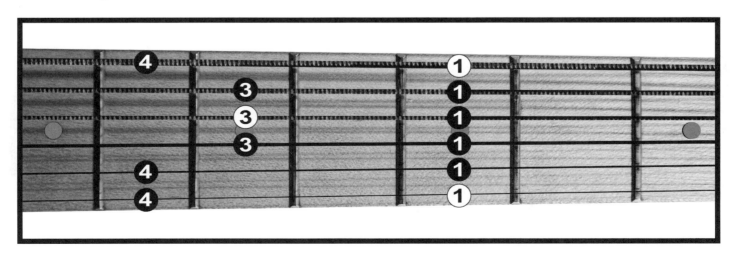

Minor Pentatonic Scale
1st Position Key of "A"

SCALE PROFESSOR

Minor pentatonic scales are the most widely used scales in rock and blues music. It is a five note scale that repeats after five scale degrees back in a circle type fashion. The notes included in the A minor pentatonic scale are A-C-D-E-G. Notice that the A notes (or root notes) are in white.

Scales are your alphabet for creating leads and melodies. Just like you learned your alphabet in school and then expanded into words, sentences and complete stories you will learn scales for guitar then expand to melodies, leads and complete songs. Practice this scale with a metronome using whole, half and quarter note timing.

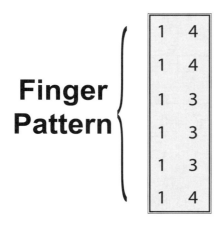

Finger Pattern

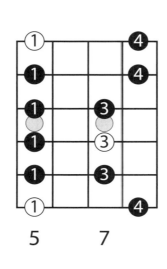

A great way to learn scales is to memorize the finger pattern (the fingers used on each string). The finger pattern for the 1st position scale is:

1 - 4, 1 - 3,1 - 3, 1 - 3, 1 - 4, 1 - 4

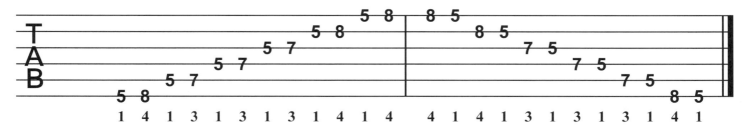

MUSIC ASSIGNMENT

After you can play this scale easily forwards and backwards, play this over the Blues in A progression and see how the notes really fit together perfectly. Start to think of this scale as a creative tool not just a group of notes forming a scale. You can even create your own melody within the confines of the scale notes by mixing the order and listening for interesting combinations.

Minor Pentatonic Lead Pattern

CD Track 41

This lead pattern comes directly from the first minor pentatonic scale. This is a great exercise to help develop coordination of your hands and help you use the scale in a creative manner. I call this the double pattern because you repeat the notes on the 5 – 2 strings. Be sure to use alternate picking consistently and build up your speed gradually. I recommend using a metronome to help gauge your progress. Tap your foot as you play the pattern to get your body clock ticking and feel the patterns rhythm. After you can play the pattern forward and backwards, play it over the Blues in A backing track. This will help you learn to play the scale as a lead application.

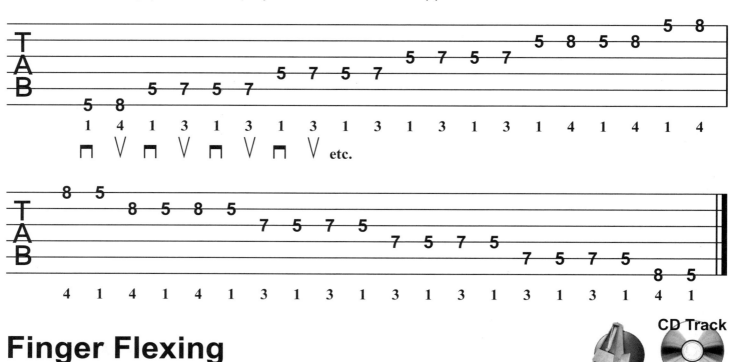

Finger Flexing

CD Track 42

This exercise follows a 5-7-6-7 fret pattern played four times on each string. Make sure to use alternate picking to generate a smooth flowing sound. Hold each note down until you are ready to pick the next and make it sound seamless. Repeat this pattern down all six strings. Practice this exercise using a metronome with quarter and eighth note timing and increase your speed a little each day.

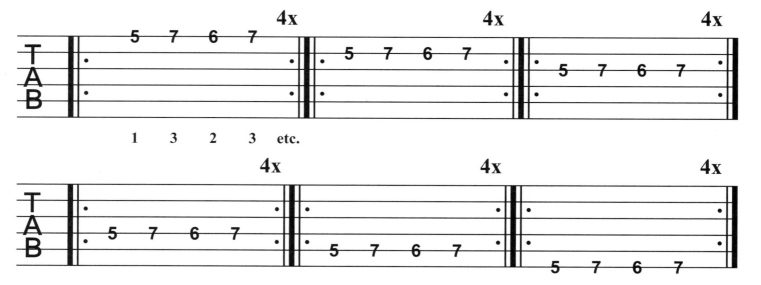

Learn Guitar 1 - Quiz 2
Once you complete this section go to RockHouseSchool.com and take the quiz to track your progress. You will receive an email with your results and suggestions.

Power Chords

CD Track
43

CHORD PROFESSOR

Power chords are constructed using only two different notes to make a very powerful sound. They are also called "5" chords because the two notes that make this chord are the root and 5th. Power chords are used in many songs and sound great when distortion is applied.

Open Power Chords

The two open power chords E5 and A5 each incorporate an open string. Follow the chord charts below to play these chords:

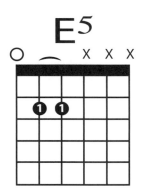

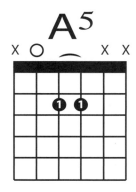

Closed Power Chords

The closed power chords F5 and Bb5 can be moved and played on any fret of the guitar. I've included a chart that tells you the name of these chords as you move them up the neck. Follow the chord chart to play these chords across the neck.

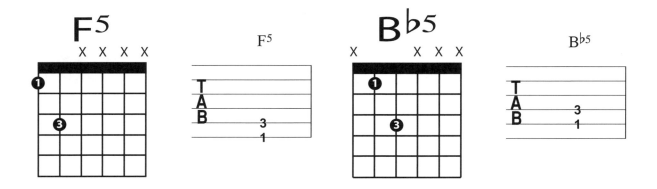

Power Chord Name Chart

Name -	F^5	$F\#^5$	G^5	$G\#^5$	A^5	$A\#^5$	B^5	C^5	$C\#^5$	D^5	$D\#^5$	E^5
Fret -	1	2	3	4	5	6	7	8	9	10	11	12
Name -	Bb^5	B^5	C^5	$C\#^5$	D^5	$D\#^5$	E^5	F^5	$F\#^5$	G^5	$G\#^5$	A^5

Below are a few examples of playing closed power chords at different frets on the neck:

G^5 A^5 B^5 C^5 D^5 E^5

```
T|--------------------------||-------------------------------|
A|--------------------------||-------------------------------|
B|--5-----7-----9-----------||--5-----7-----9----------------|
 |--3-----5-----7-----------||--3-----5-----7----------------|
```

MUSIC ASSIGNMENT

Practice changing from chord to chord so you are prepared to use these power chords in the next lesson and be sure to memorize the chord names too.

Power Chord Rhythm

Hit it Hard

You will use the open power chords and the F closed power chord moved to the 3rd fret (G chord) in this rhythm. All the strums are down. This is very characteristic of rock songs to get a heavy driving sound. Once you feel comfortable playing this chord progression, play it along with the backing track.

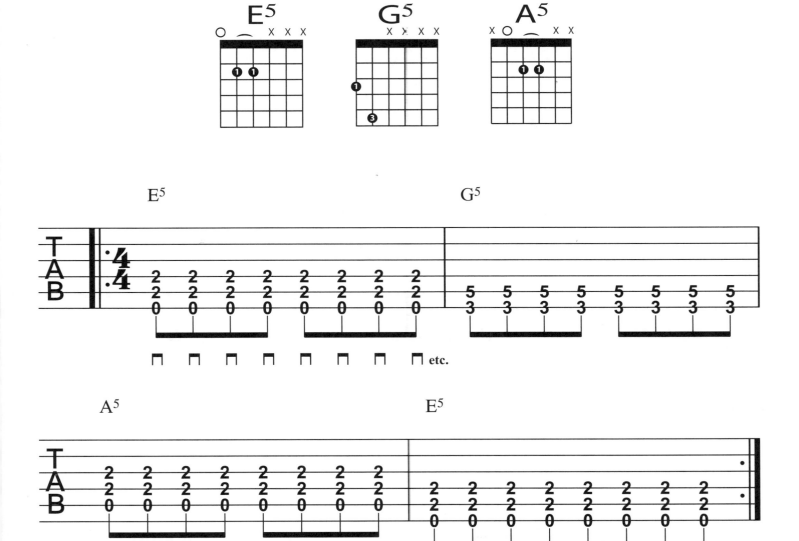

41

Major Open Chords

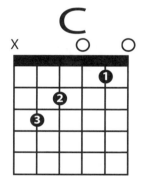

CHORD PROFESSOR

Now it's time to learn some important major chords. These chords are used in countless songs in all styles of music. A few of these will be challenging and may take some time to master, so be patient.

B

C

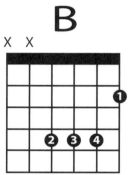

F

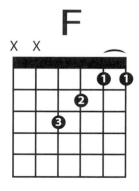

G

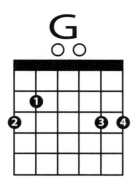

Cadd⁹

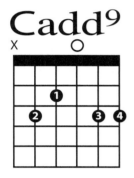

The Ghost Strum

It's very important when strumming to keep your right hand and arm moving down up consistently. There will be times when you're not striking the strings, but your arm and pick will be going over the strings to keep the steady down up motion. These strums are "Ghost Strums." Look at the following diagram to see how the "Ghost Strum" is used in a strum pattern. Practice this strumming pattern while holding down the G open chord.

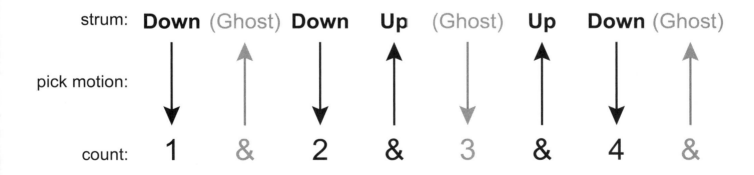

strum: **Down** (Ghost) **Down** **Up** (Ghost) **Up** **Down** (Ghost)

pick motion:

count: 1 & 2 & 3 & 4 &

Song Rhythm

A Day at the Beach

This chord progression has been used in many songs. There will be common fingers held down from chord to chord. The following chord diagrams show which fingers to leave down to make the changes easier:

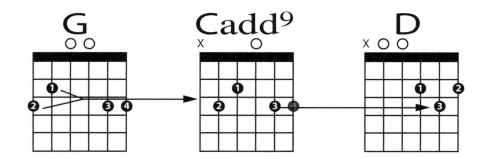

Play the complete song below. The strum pattern is repeated two times for the G chord and once for the Cadd9 and D. The pattern is the pattern you learned using the ghost strum. Make sure to play this progression over the bass and drum backing track.

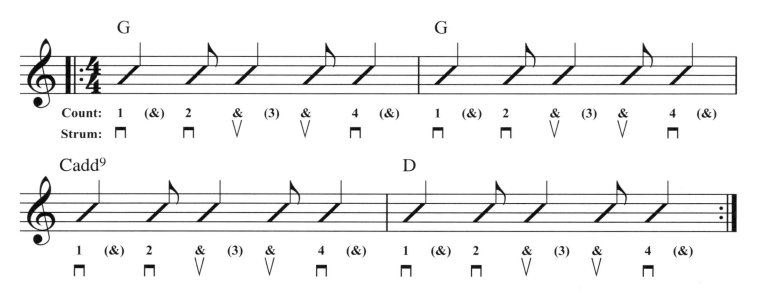

MUSIC ASSIGNMENT

The three chords in this lesson are very popular chords that are used for many rock and pop hits. Take these chords and switch the order around to make your own progression. There are many different ways you can coordinate these three chords into a progression to make a unique sound. Experiment and create your own masterpiece.

Classical Melody - Ode to Joy

CD Track

49-50

Here is a great classical melody by Beethoven. In this song there is a tie that connects a quarter and eighth note. Pay close attention to the count below the staff for these measures, the next note will be pick on an up beat or the & count. I've included the chords for the song above the staff. Once you have learned the melody, play the rhythm by strumming the chords above the staff along with the melody.

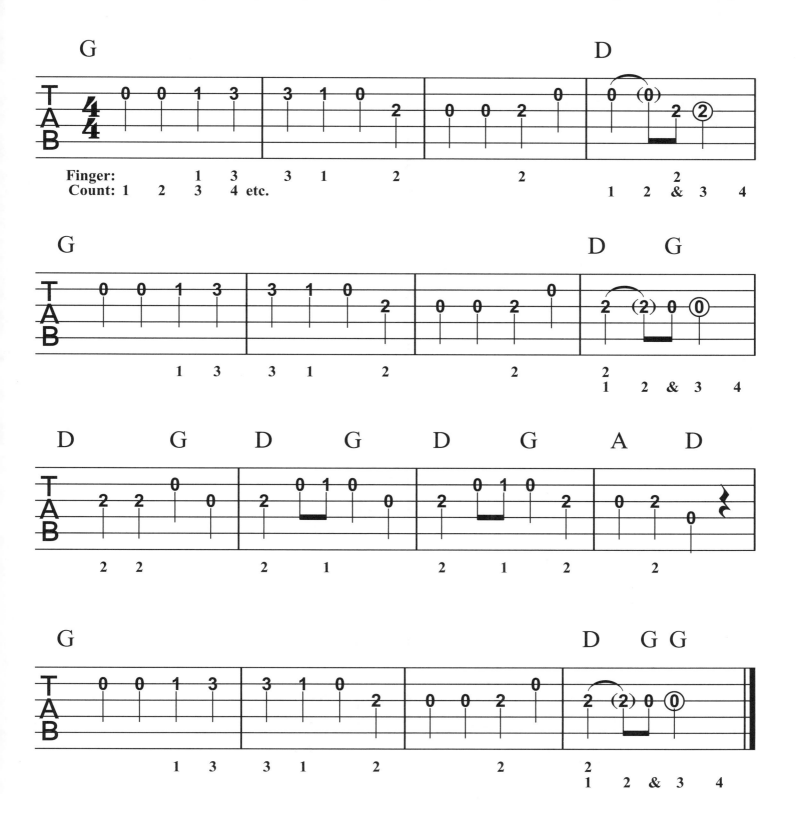

Minor Pentatonic Scale

Positions 2 & 3

SCALE PROFESSOR

Like the 1st position scale these scales contain the notes A-C-D-E-G played at different places on the neck. Use alternate picking as you build up speed and memorize the location of the root notes (in white) within each scale pattern.

Finger Pattern

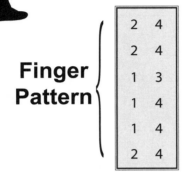

2nd Position

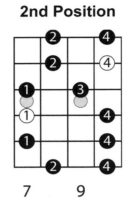

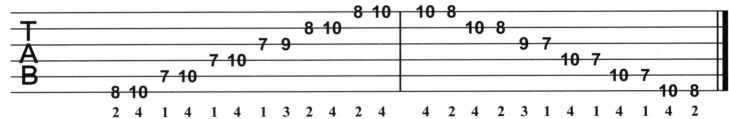

Finger Pattern

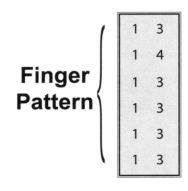

3rd Position

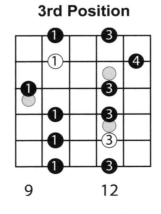

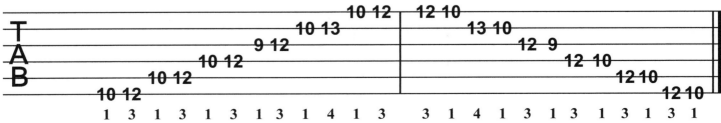

Minor Pentatonic Lead Pattern

Positions 2 & 3

Apply the double lead pattern you learned earlier to the 2nd and 3rd position scales. Double the notes on the 5th - 2nd strings going forward and backwards. Make sure to use alternate picking.

2nd Position

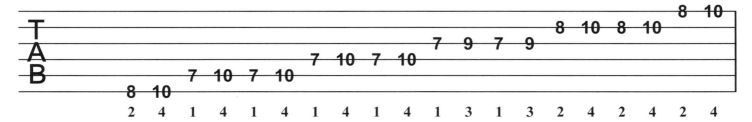

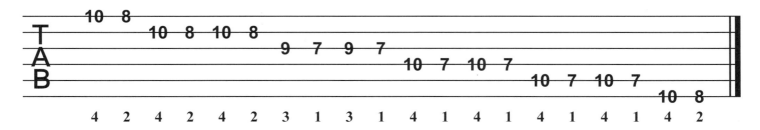

3rd Position

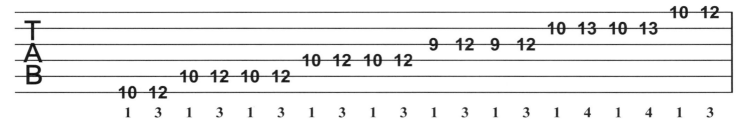

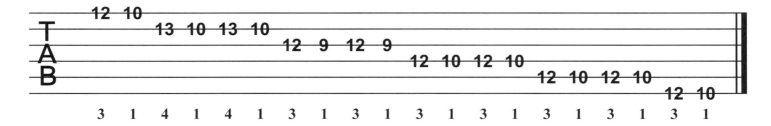

![Guitar player silhouette]

MUSIC ASSIGNMENT

Once you're comfortable playing this pattern practice along with a metronome. Start at a slow tempo and increase speed gradually each time you practice. Concentrate on technique, picking each note clear and distinct, with consistent alternate picking. Another thing that will make this pattern more challenging is to play each note twice as you play through the sequence.

Song Riff

This is a picked song riff. Hold down the fingers for each group of four eighth notes and let the notes ring together. The last four notes are a riff that brings you back to the beginning to repeat.

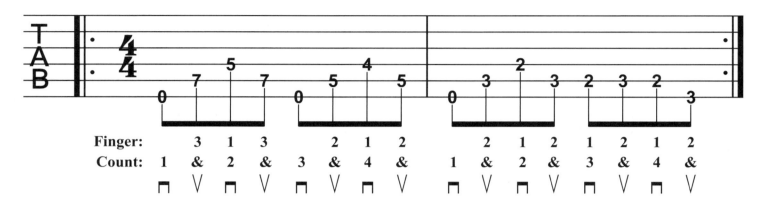

Combining Major & Minor Chords

CD Track
54-55

Blue Velvet

The strum pattern for this rhythm is: down, down, down-up-down-up. Play this strumming pattern once for each chord. There will be common fingers held down from chord to chord that will make the transitions easier. Keep your hand, arm and shoulder loose and relaxed at all times. Never tense or tighten up your strumming arm. Once you can play this chord progression smoothly, changing from chord to chord, use the backing track and play along with the bass and drums.

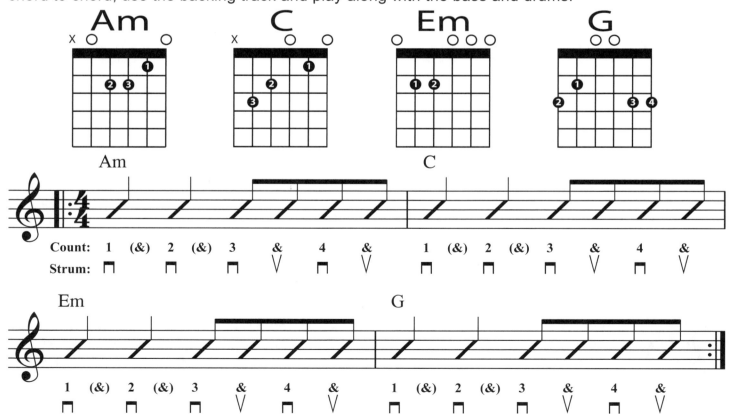

Song Progression

Street of Dreams

Look for the common fingers that can be held down from chord to chord like the previous lesson. The strum pattern is: down, down, down, down-up once for each chord.

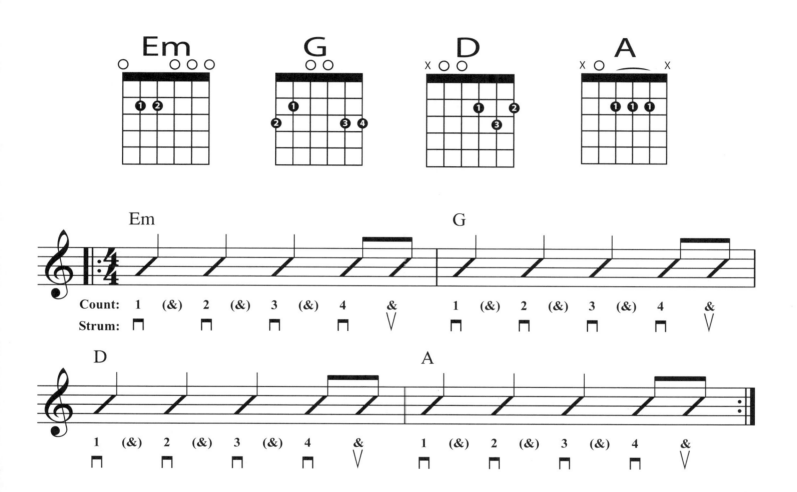

MUSIC ASSIGNMENT

As you learn more chords and strum patterns you will be able to start creating your own song progressions. By simply changing the order of chords or varying the strum pattern you can drastically change the sound of a song progression. Play the progression above with the chords in a different order as follows G - Em - A - D and see how it sounds like a new song. Next play the strum pattern from Blue Velvet with the song progression in this lesson and see how it gives it a different feel.

Minor Pentatonic Triplet Lead Pattern

Eighth notes subdivide a beat in half an even number breakdown of two. Triplets subdivide a beat into threes. For every one beat, you will play three notes. Count triplets as follows:

One - Trip - Let - **Two** - Trip - Let - **Three** - Trip - Let - **Four** - Trip - Let

Play triplets with the minor pentatonic scales following along with the tablature. Count along as you play to help learn the timing. Apply this pattern over the basic blues progression you previously learned in this program.

1st Position

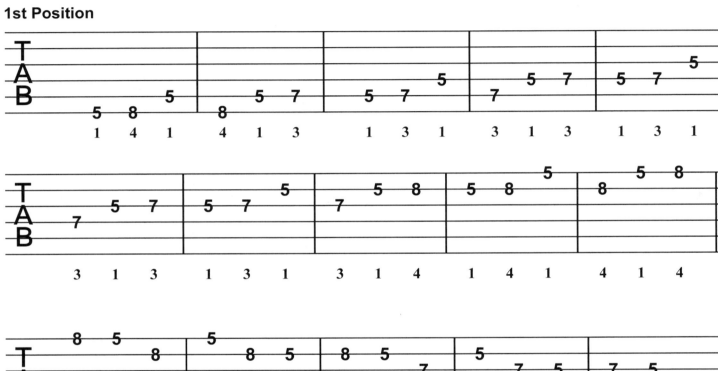

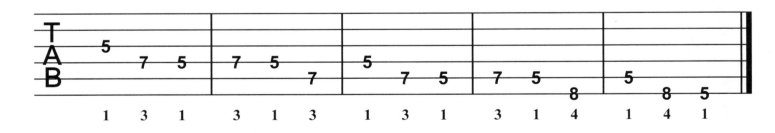

2nd Position

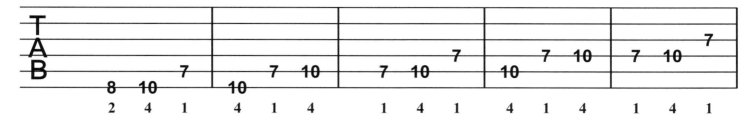

3rd Position

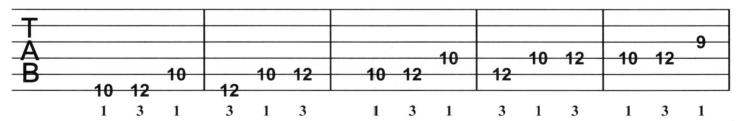

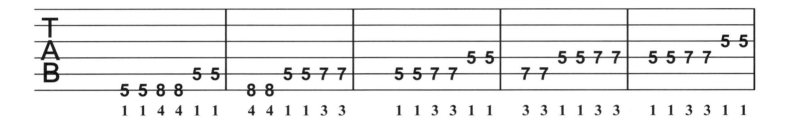

MUSIC ASSIGNMENT

Vary this pattern and play each note of this triplet lead pattern twice. Next, transpose this pattern forwards and backwards with all three scale positions.

Practice Tips

To ensure constant progress and high motivation you have to develop practice habits that will keep you interested and challenged. Here are a few tips:

Practice Consistently - You need to give your fingers a chance to gain muscle memory. Practice every day even if it is for a short amount of time, be consistent.

Practice Area - Have a practice spot set up so you can have privacy to focus on your playing. It is a great idea to have a music stand to help position your music so you can sit comfortably.

Practice Schedule - Set a scheduled practice time each day and make this a routine. Other times in the day you can play for fun and jam a little.

Power Chord Rhythms

Gear Shifter

The following rhythms contain all power chords. The strum patterns combine eighth and quarter notes.

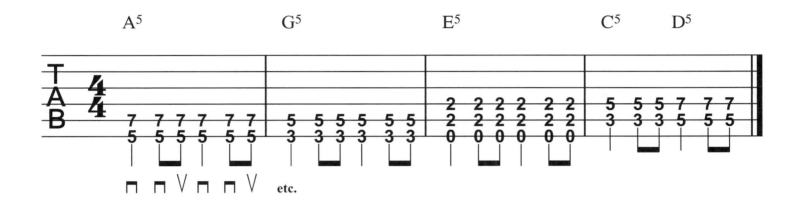

Unbreakable

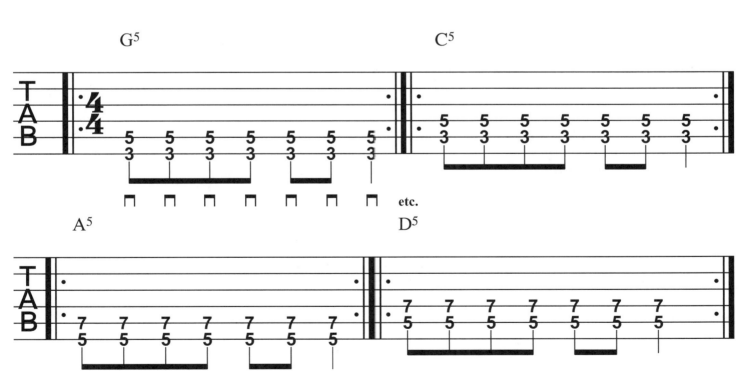

Finger Flexing #2

Here is an exercise to develop the coordination of both hands. Use the same finger and fret number when you play this exercise lining your fingers up in a one finger per fret manner. Hold your first finger down on each string, this will help to open up your hand and develop a reach. Repeat each measure four times using alternate picking. Build up speed gradually. Once you feel comfortable playing this pattern across all 6 strings, do the same pattern playing each note twice, then do it again but play each note three times using the picking pattern *down-up-down* to *up-down-up* going across the strings Use a metronome to help you gauge your progress. Increase the speed a notch every day to effectively improve your skill.

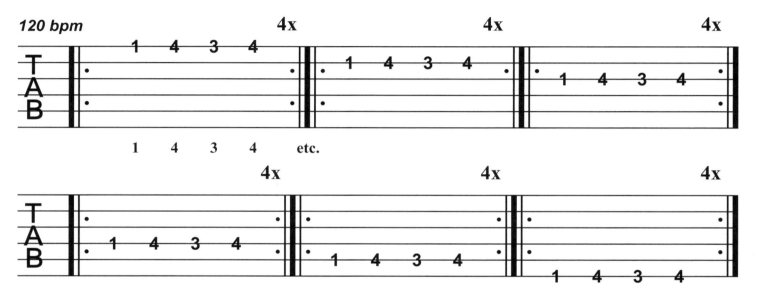

Lead Techniques – Bending

CD Track 63

Bending is the most widely used technique in modern guitar. It is a great way to add soul and emotional dimension to your notes. To bend a note simply pick it and push your finger up while keeping the pressure pressed down. By doing this you alter and control the note's pitch. An arrow above a note indicates a bend, a "full" at the end of the arrow indicates to bend the note up one whole step in pitch. When fretting the bend keep your other fingers down on the string to help give strength, control and accuracy. Once you get familiar with bending, apply the bending techniques to the minor pentatonic scales. Make sure to use all the fingers before the note you're bending, to help push up the bend and control it. The only time you should use one finger to bend is when you're bending with your first finger.

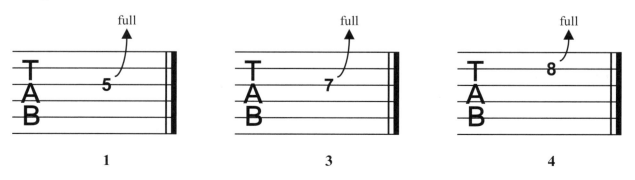

Single Note Riff Rhythm

Here is a single note riff rhythm that has a blues rock sound. The pattern stays the same throughout the rhythm so memorize the first measure before going through the whole song. Be sure to play this with the bass and drum backing track.

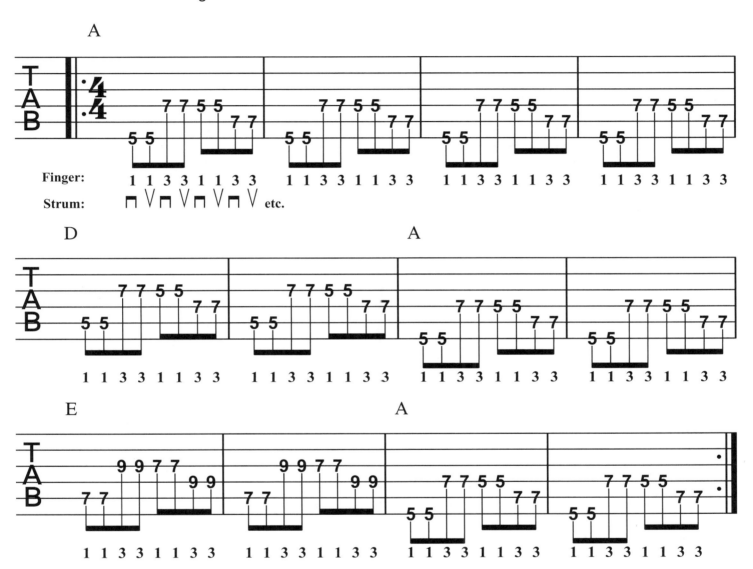

MUSIC ASSIGNMENT

This rhythm can be played with the shuffle feel used in the Blues in A lesson. Apply the shuffle feel to make this rhythm sound more like the blues.

Lead Techniques – Hammer Ons

Hammer ons are a widely used lead guitar technique. A curved line connecting two tablature notes with an "H" on top indicates a hammer on. Pick the first note; the second note will be sounded by pushing your finger down in a hammer like fashion to make the sound resonate. In the following exercise only pick the first note on each string:

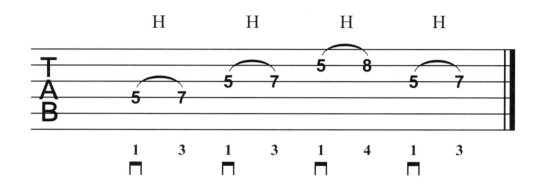

The second exercise is applied to the minor pentatonic scale. This pattern starts on the 6th string and goes down in three string intervals to the 1st string.

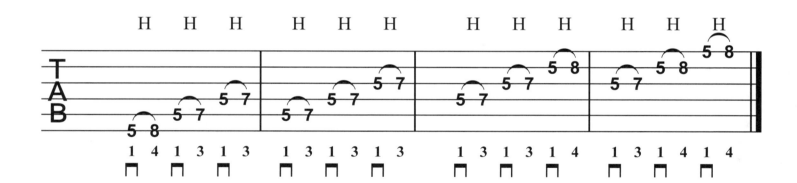

MUSIC ASSIGNMENT

Once you feel comfortable playing hammer ons, apply them to the other minor pentatonic scales. This will help you master this technique and use the scales in a lead application.

Complete Blues Lead

This lead incorporates all the lead techniques you've learned applied to the minor pentatonic scales. There is no timing notation applied to this lead, add your own creative variations. Play the lead over the full band backing track. The chord names above the tab staff are there for a reference to tell you where the chord changes are:

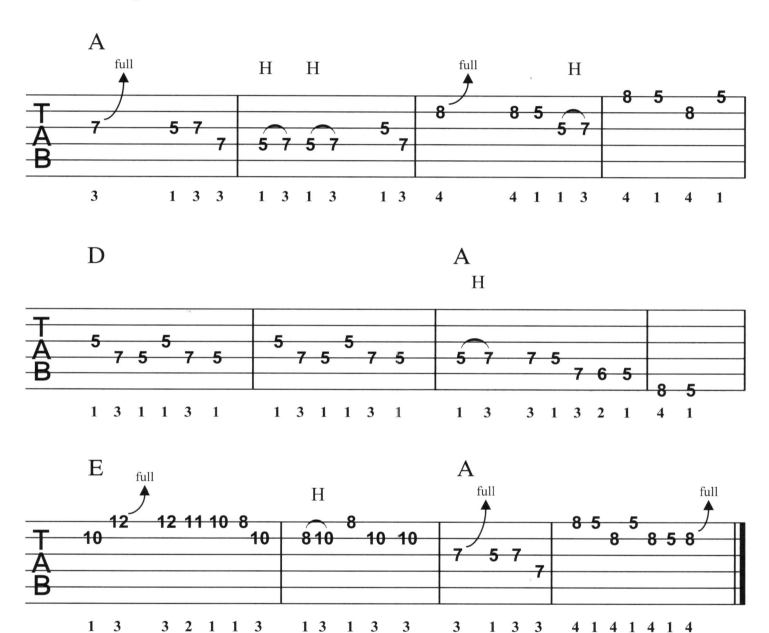

MUSIC ASSIGNMENT

Once you are able to play this entire lead over the full band backing track take this to the next level and create your own lead. Start by just changing the notes in each measure a little bit to make your own riffs. Then put them together and make your own lead. Remember that the entire lead comes from the notes of the minor pentatonic scales you already know.

Open Chord Progression

Rock Climbing

This progression contains chords that you have previously played and should have memorized by now. Follow the rhythm count below the staff for the strum pattern.

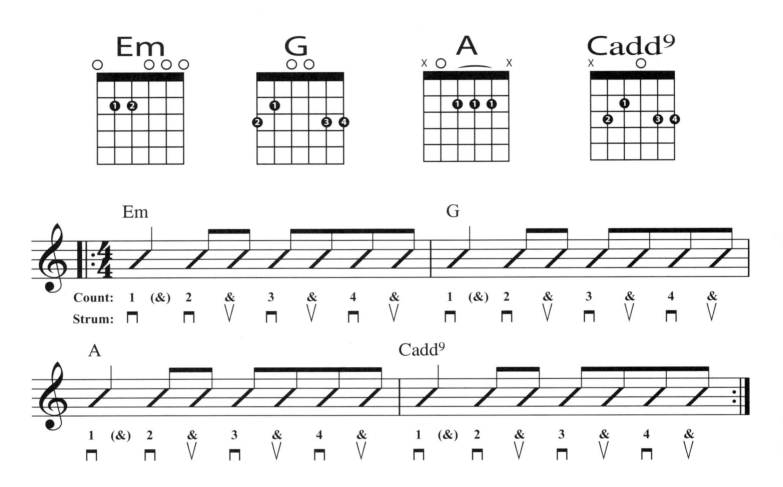

Palm Mute

To palm mute lightly touch the side of your picking hand on the strings, just where they come off the bridge to create a muffled, tight sound as you play. Be careful not to go too far away from the bridge, because you'll get a deadened sound instead of muted. Palm muting will allow you to dynamically control your overall sound. A "P.M." followed by a dotted line indicates palm muting on the staff below:

P.M. -

```
T
A
B  3    3    3    3    3    3    3    3
   1    1    1    1    1    1    1    1
```

Power Chord Rhythm

CD Track
72-73

Rockit Center

This rhythm is presented two ways. The first is strummed eight times down each chord; this creates a great solid rhythm. The second example is strummed 16 times per chord with alternate strumming: this gives the rhythm a heavier sound. After you can play the chord changes easily add the palm muting technique to the rhythm to create a chunkier, rock sound. Play along with the backing track and apply this rhythm. Apply the muting technique taught in the previous lesson to this progression. Mute one chord, unmute the next and try different variations. This will help you to get comfortable and understand how to use this technique effectively with progressions.

Example 1

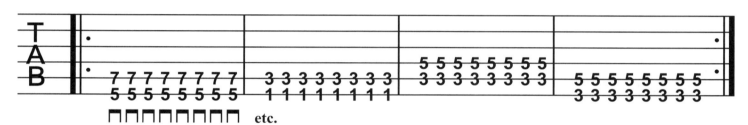

Example 2

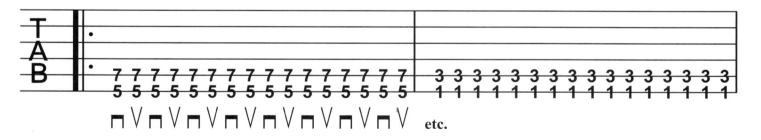

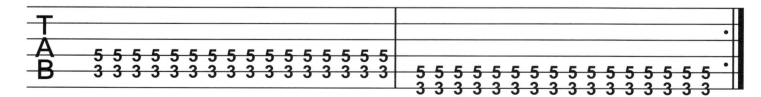

Building Your Pick Speed

Alternate Picking

In this exercise there are a series of sequences combined to create a complete picking routine. Follow the tablature with consistent alternate picking through all three sequences.

3rd & 4th Strings

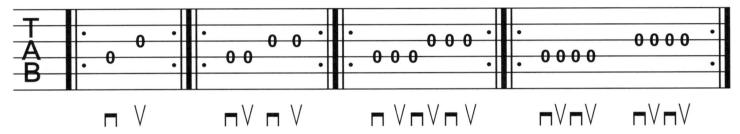

2nd & 4th Strings

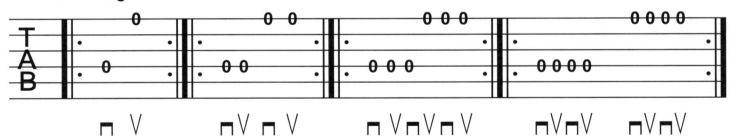

1st & 4th Strings

MUSIC ASSIGNMENT

Use a metronome with this exercise to gauge your progress and develop better timing habits. Start at 65 bpm and increase your speed in small increments each day. Pick your notes clear and hard.

Lead Riffs

Single note riffs can be used in leads or rhythm sections in songs. These riffs are lead riffs. Most riffs come from scales; these examples come directly from the 1st position A minor pentatonic scale. Once you have these memorized, create your own riffs using the scales. Write your riffs in tablature and build a collection of your own.

Riff 1

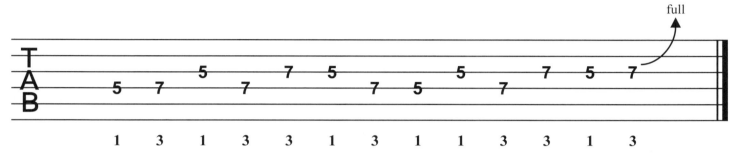

Riff 2

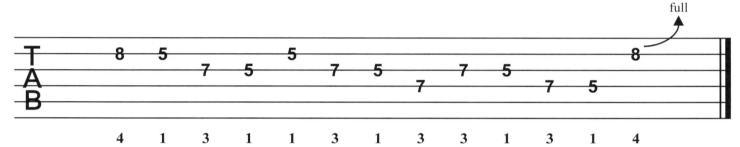

MUSIC ASSIGNMENT

Create a riff from each of the minor pentatonic scales. You can even use open strings when making riffs. Be creative and write your examples on a blank tablature sheets. If you need blank tablature paper visit RockHouseSchool.com.

Using the Metronome to Practice

As you progress as a guitarist you can use the metronome in your daily practice to help keep a steady rhythm and gauge your progress. Here are a few metronome practice tips that will help you use this tool effectively.

1. When starting to learn a new song set the metronome at a slow tempo where you can play the entire piece through without making mistakes.

2. Gradually build your speed by increasing the BPM (beats per minute) on the metronome a few numbers each day.

3. As you play with the metronome try not to focus on it too much. Sense the feel of the click and concentrate on the song you are playing.

More Minor Chords

CHORD PROFESSOR

Notice that the Bm and Cm chords have the same fingering only played in different frets. The Fm and Gm chords contain a first finger bar and also use identical fingerings.

What makes a minor chord sad is the 3rd degree gets flatted (or lowered) one half step. To hear the difference between major and minor chords clearly, strum the E major then E minor chords back-to-back. The only note different is the 3rd string, this makes the chord sound major or minor.

Bm
X X
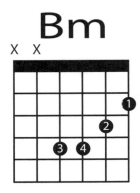

Cm
X X
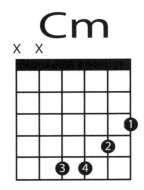

Dm
X O O
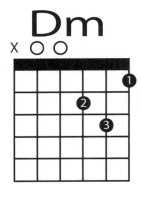

Fm

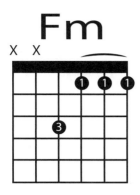

Gm

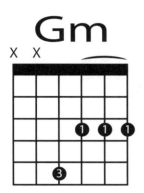

MUSIC ASSIGNMENT

Practice changing from chord to chord to challenge your fingers. Some good combinations are from B minor to D minor, from C minor to G minor and from F minor to A minor. Practice until you can finger these chord changes easily and quickly so you can use them in song progressions.

Vibrato

Vibrato is a rapid, slight variation in a notes pitch producing a stronger or richer tone. This is achieved on the guitar by shaking your hand in very small rapid movements after you pick a note. This creates a pulsating effect similar to a singer's vibrato. Make sure not to bend the notes pitch. Vibrato is designated by a squiggly line above a note. Play the two notes to the right and apply the vibrato technique.

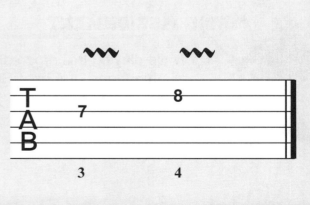

Minor Song Progression

Black Pearl

The strum pattern used here is the same you previously learned that incorporated the "Ghost Strum" technique. There will be some common fingers from chord to chord. Play this progression over the bass and drum backing track. Notice that the Em chord uses an alternate fingering to make changing from chord to chord easier.

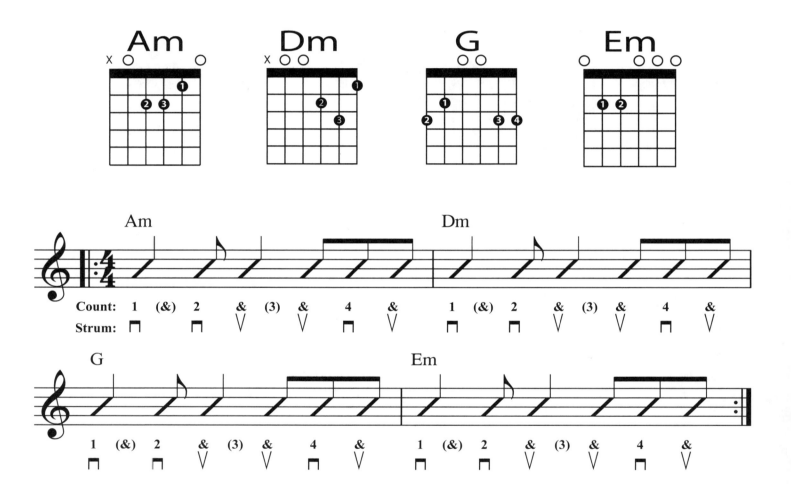

MUSIC ASSIGNMENT

While playing this progression over the backing track of bass and drums, vary your combinations of Ghost Strum and strumming. This will help you to create new patterns and a more distinct style of your own.

Finger Picking Basics

Learning to play guitar picking with your fingers will not only help you play classical style music but you can use this technique to play any genre of music. Many guitarists that use a pick also add a hybrid pick and finger technique to give a new dimension to their sound. Start by learning the basics of finger picking; in the future you can experiment using this in many applications.

The fingers on your picking hand are referenced by the following symbols: p = thumb, i = index finger, m = middle finger, a = ring finger. Look at the pictures below to see the proper posture for the finger picking style as well as the picking hand finger symbols:

 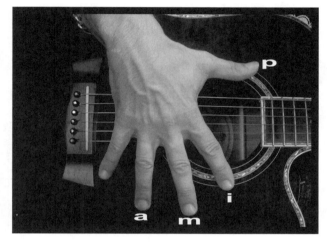

Next, play through the example to the right with the open first four strings to get the feel for using your fingers to pick. In the next lesson you will be playing an entire song using finger picking, so get excited!

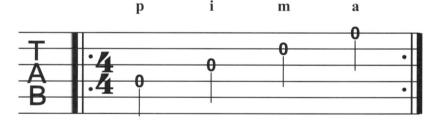

Finger Picking Progression

CD Track
79-80

Here is a finger picking song using the A minor to E minor progression. On the E minor chord the pattern will be 6-3-2-1-2-3 and the fingering will be p-i-m-a-m-i and on the A minor chord the pattern will be 5-3-2-1-2-3 using the same right hand fingering. Try to use this pattern with all the other chords you've learned and even make your own picking patterns by varying your fingers. Be creative and have some fun!

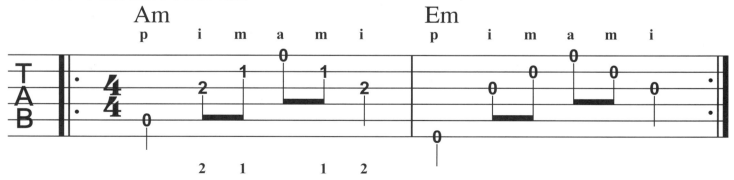

Minor Pentatonic Scale

Positions 4 & 5

SCALE PROFESSOR

In this lesson you will learn the last two positions of the minor pentatonic scale. There are two places on the neck that each position can be played. If you have an acoustic guitar that does not have access to the higher frets play only the lower fret variation. Memorize the finger pattern for each scale and use alternate picking.

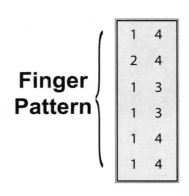

Finger Pattern

1	4
2	4
1	3
1	3
1	4
1	4

4th Position

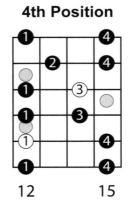

12   15

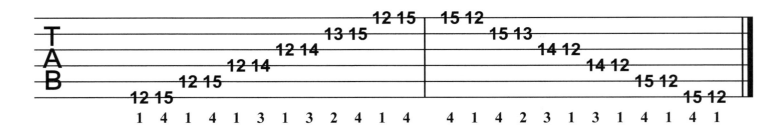

1 4 1 4 1 3 1 3 2 4 1 4   4 1 4 2 3 1 3 1 4 1 4 1

4th Position (Open)

3   3   2   2 1 3   3   3   3 1 2   2   3   3

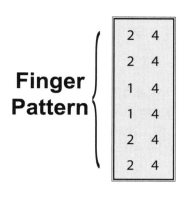

Finger Pattern

2	4
2	4
1	4
1	4
2	4
2	4

5th Position

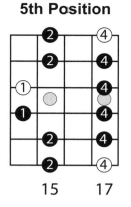

15   17

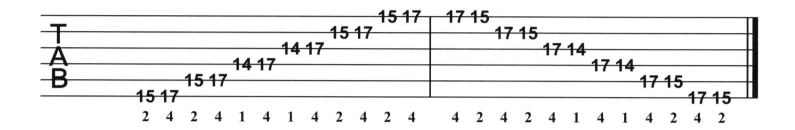

```
                                                    15 17   17 15
                                          15 17              17 15
                                 14 17                            17 14
                        14 17                                          17 14
               15 17                                                        17 15
      15 17                                                                      17 15
```
2 4 2 4 1 4 1 4 2 4 2 4   4 2 4 2 4 1 4 1 4 2 4 2

5th Position (Lower Octave)

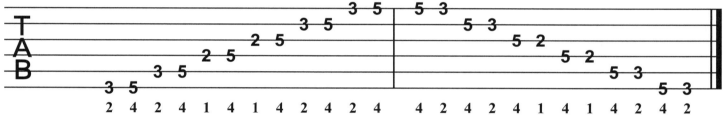

```
                                                    3  5    5  3
                                          3  5              5  3
                                 2  5                            5  2
                        2  5                                          5  2
               3  5                                                        5  3
      3  5                                                                      5  3
```
2 4 2 4 1 4 1 4 2 4 2 4   4 2 4 2 4 1 4 1 4 2 4 2

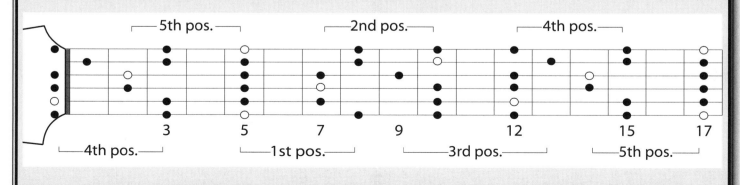

Minor Pentatonic Scales - Full Neck

You have learned all five minor pentatonic scale patterns in the key of "A." All these patterns have the same notes, A – C – D – E and G played at different spots across the neck. Below is a full neck diagram of all five minor pentatonic scales in the key of "A." You can clearly see how the scales connect together on this diagram.

Applying the Pentatonic Scale

This lesson will help to ignite your creative senses! I'm going to start you off and create a melody using the minor pentatonic scales that can be played over the power chord progression learned earlier in the program. The melody below contains riffs from all five minor pentatonic scales, as you play this melody notice which scale each riff was created from. Use the full band backing track to play this lead over to get the feel of playing lead guitar.

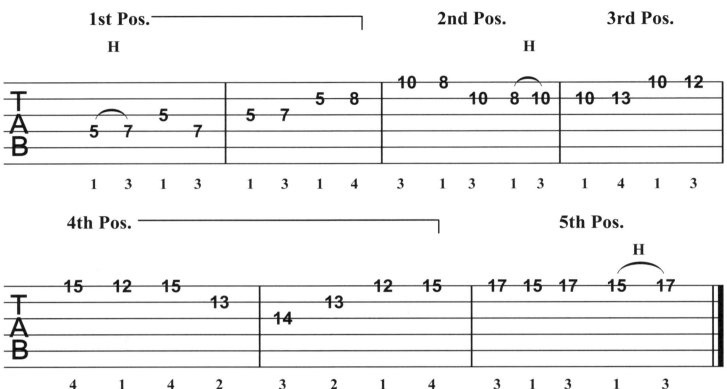

MUSIC ASSIGNMENT

As you learn to improvise you will use scales as creative tools and begin crafting riffs and leads. You will gather a collection of your personal riffs, I call this your "Bag of Tricks." The more leads and riffs you know the better you will be able to improvise. Your assignment is to create a riff from each of the five minor pentatonic scales you have learned. Start by playing the scales forwards and backwards then mix up the notes in your own unique way. This will not be easy at first, but keep at it and it will get easier every time you try. As you create your riffs always write them down so they will always be just a glance away. If you need blank tablature paper, go to RockHouseSchool.com.

Root Notes

The root note is the most important note of a scale; it is also the name of the scale and at times referred to as the "Tonic" or "Tonal Center." In an A minor pentatonic scale, the A note would be the root note. In this lesson take all five minor pentatonic scales and locate every root note within each pattern. Look at the diagrams on the next page and you'll see the root notes depicted.

4th Position	5th Position	1st Position	2nd Position

```
T ---------------------|-----------5---|-----------5---|---------------|
A -------------2-------|-----2---------|---------------|-----------10--|
B ---0-----------------|---------------|-------7-------|-------7-------|
                       |-----5---------|-----5---------|
```

3rd Position	4th Position	5th Position	1st Position

```
T -----------10--|---------------|-----------17--|-----------17--|
A ---------------|-------14------|-----14--------|---------------|
B -----12--------|-----12--------|---------------|-------19------|
                 |               |-------17------|-----17--------|
```

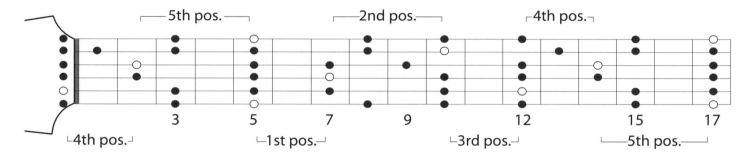

5th pos.   2nd pos.   4th pos.

3   5   7   9   12   15   17

4th pos.   1st pos.   3rd pos.   5th pos.

MUSIC ASSIGNMENT

Play only the root notes for each scale pattern up the neck across all five scale positions as quickly as you can forwards and backwards. This is a great exercise to memorize where the root notes are in each scale pattern. When creating leads or melodies, these are great notes to start or stop on.

CD Track

84

Song Riff #2

A riff can be the main hook for a song. The following is an example of a simple but catchy song riff. Pick each finger up after it has been picked.

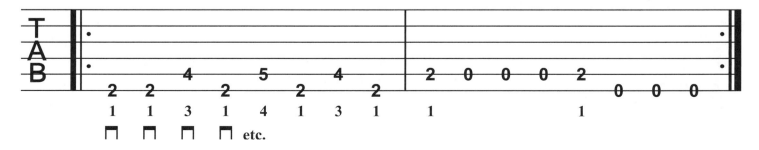

```
T ||:-------------------------------------|-----------------------------------:||
A ||:-------------------------------------|-----------------------------------:||
B ||:-------4-----5-----4----------------|---2---0---0---0---2---------------:||
   ||:--2---2--------2-----2---2----------|---------------------------0---0---0:||
```

1   1   3   1   4   1   3   1   1   1

⊓ ⊓ ⊓ ⊓ etc.

Lead Techniques – Pull Offs

CD Track 85

Pull offs are the opposite of hammer ons. On the staff below there are two tab notes with a curved line (or slur) connecting them. The "P" on top is the symbol for the pull off. Put both fingers down then pull off (snap off) your 3rd finger to sound the second note, one pick will sound two notes.

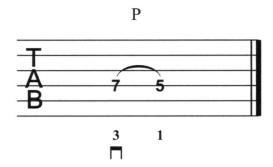

Now play pull offs in a simple pattern from the minor pentatonic scale to get started.

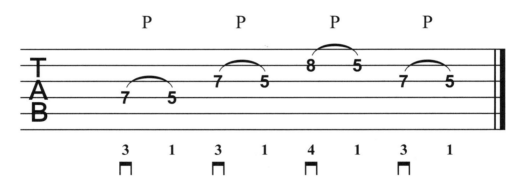

The next exercise is applied to the complete minor pentatonic scale. Start on the 1st string and go down in a three string sequence pulling off the second note on each string.

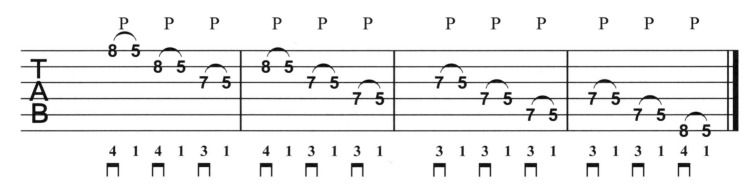

MUSIC ASSIGNMENT

Once you have mastered playing pull offs with the 1st position minor pentatonic scale, apply pull offs to all five minor pentatonic scales using the three string sequence from this lesson. Play along with a metronome or any backing track that is in the key of "A" from this program.

Single Note Riff Rhythm #2

The High Road

Here is another single note riff rhythm. This one is a little more challenging because you must use your 4th finger. This rhythm has a repeating pattern so memorize the first measure before trying the entire song. Make sure to play this over the bass and drum backing track.

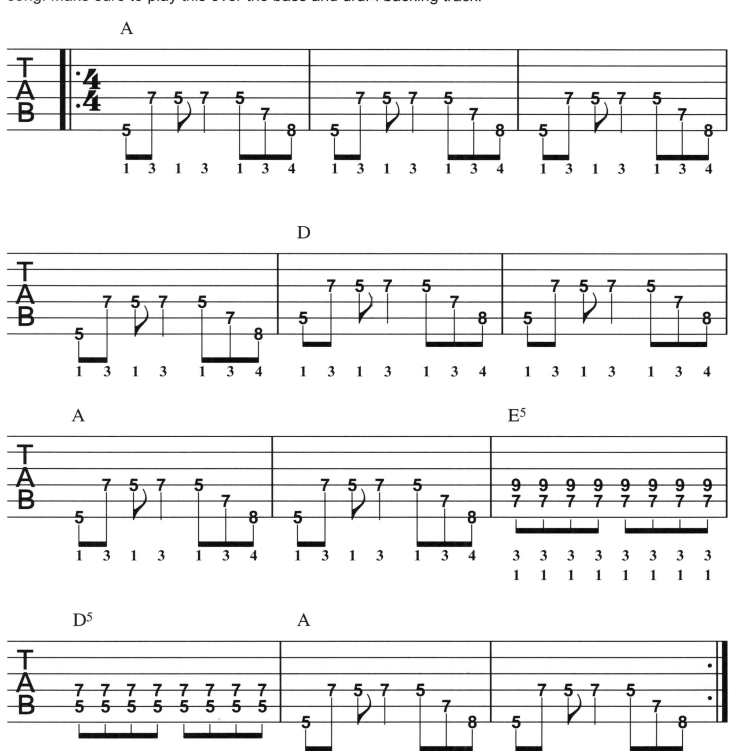

Dotted Notes

The dot after a note increases the duration of the note by half of its original value. If the basic note is a half note (2 beats), the dotted note is 3 beats or counts. A dotted quarter note would receive 1 ½ beats or counts. The Star Spangled Banner melody below will be using both dotted half and quarter notes.

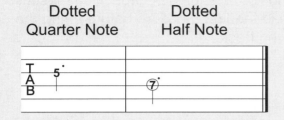

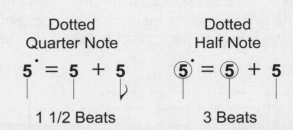

Dotted Quarter Note: $5\dot{} = 5 + 5$ 1 1/2 Beats

Dotted Half Note: $⑤\dot{} = ⑤ + 5$ 3 Beats

The Star Spangled Banner

CD Track 88-89

This great melody has been played by countless musicians. One of the most famous is the version that Jimi Hendrix played with heavy distortion and whammy bar tricks. Learn the basic melody and after you have this under your fingers, experiment and try to make your own version. Add some distortion to it or use techniques like hammer ons, pull offs and bends. Be creative!

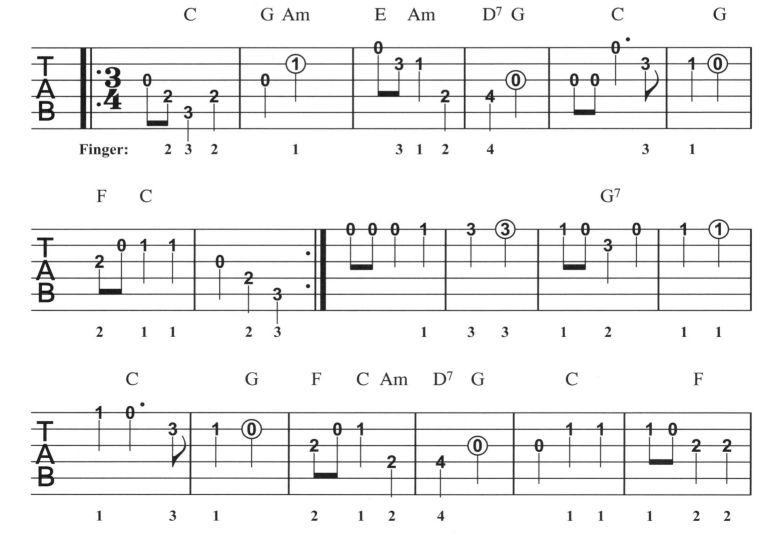

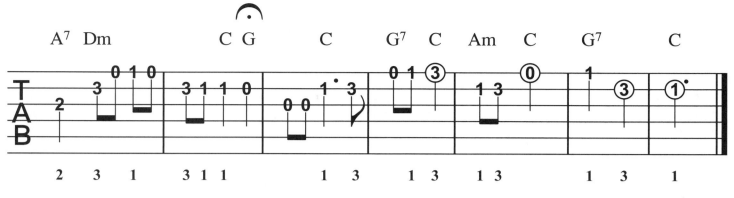

⌢· : **Fermata-** Hold the note longer than the written time value.

Syncopated Rhythm

Jacob's Ladder

Here is another strum pattern that can be applied to any of the progressions in this book. This strum pattern has an "up" syncopation feel. Pay attention to the counting below the staff to help you understand the rhythm easily:

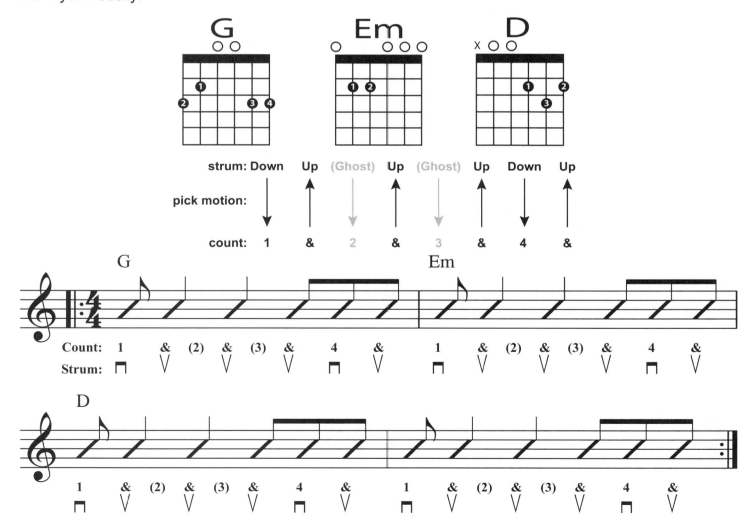

Lead Techniques – Hammer Pull Offs

Now combine the hammer on and pull off technique together in three note groupings within the first position minor pentatonic scale. The technique is done in one swift movement, one pick followed by a hammer pull off sequence. Three notes are sounded with one pick:

The second example is a pattern applied to the 1st position minor pentatonic scale. This combines the hammer pull off technique with single notes.

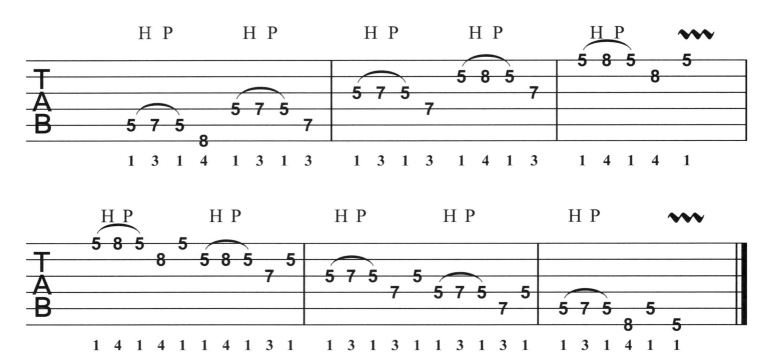

MUSIC ASSIGNMENT

Once you feel comfortable playing the hammer pull off technique apply this pattern to the other four minor pentatonic scales. Play along with a metronome or any backing track that is in the key of "A" from this program. This will help you get a good understanding of how to apply this technique as a lead.

74

Complete Rhythm & Lead

This is a classic rock rhythm and lead. Practice the rhythm first: it consists of mostly power chords. Play the rhythm over the bass and drum backing track. Next, move on to the lead and work through this section by section. Once you feel comfortable playing the lead through from start to finish play it over the full band backing track and put it all together.

Rhythm

Lead

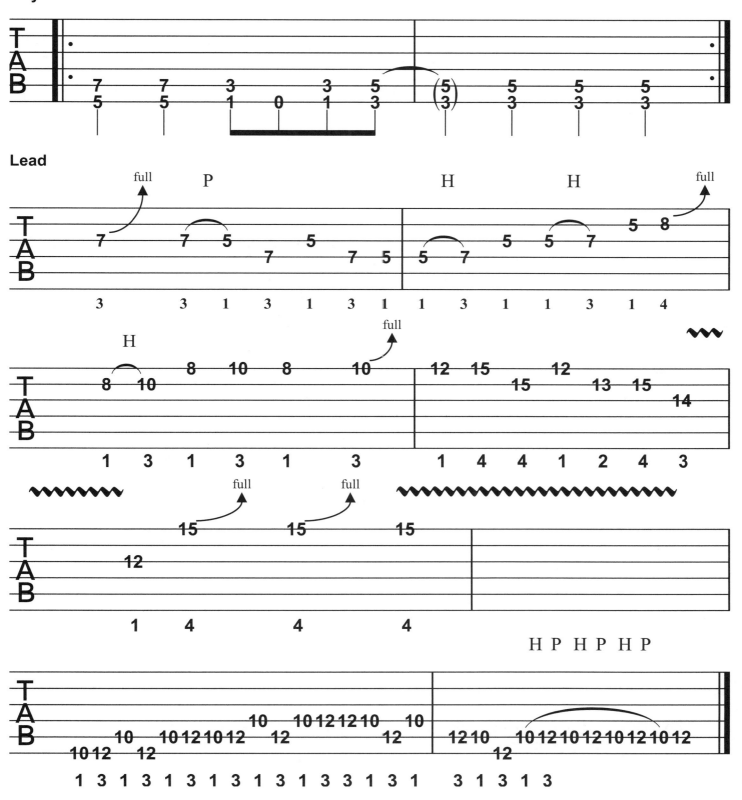

75

Musical Words

Action - Height of the strings from the fret board to the string itself.

Beat - The regular pulse of music which may be dictated by a metronome, or by the accents in music.

Bridge - The bridge is located on the body of the guitar and transfers sound from the strings to the body of the guitar. This can be held in place by screws or string tension.

Body - The main section of the instrument where the bridge and tailpiece are located.

Chord - The sounding of three or more notes simultaneously.

Fretboard or Fingerboard - The area on top of the neck that you press the string upon to create a note or frequency.

Flat - An accidental symbol placed to the left of a note, indicating that its pitch should be lowered by a half step.

Fret - The metal strips along your fretboard. They come in a variety of sizes. For example, small, medium, medium-jumbo, or jumbo. The size depends on what a player likes best.

Headstock - Top of the instrument where the tuners or machine heads are located.

Interval - The distance between two pitches.

Machine Head - A device to control the tension of the strings. With a slight turn of the machine head, the player can tighten or loosen the tension to raise or lower the pitch of the string until it is in tune.

Melody - A succession of single tones containing rhythm and pitches arranged as a musical shape.

Neck - The middle of the guitar where the strings are stretched over the fretboard.

Nut - Piece of plastic or bone between the headstock and fretboard. Guides the strings from the fretboard to the tuners on the headstock.

Pickguard - Piece of material placed on the body of the guitar to protect it from pick scratches.

Pickup - Device that takes the string vibration that you create and transforms it into an electronic signal. This signal is then sent to the amplifier to boost the sound.

Saddles - Piece on the bridge that holds the string in place.

Scale - A series of notes in ascending or descending order that presents the pitches of a key or mode, beginning and ending on the tonic of that key or mode.

Sharp - An accidental symbol placed to the left of a note, indicating that its pitch should be raised by a half step.

Tempo - The speed of the rhythm of a composition. Tempo is measured according to beats per minute.

Timing - The beat of musical rhythm. The controlled movement of music in time.

Triplet - Three notes of equal length that are to be performed in the duration of two notes of equal length.

Changing a String

Old guitar strings may break or lose their tone and become harder to keep in tune. You might feel comfortable at first having a teacher or someone at a music store change your strings for you, but eventually you will need to know how to do it yourself. Changing the strings on a guitar is not as difficult as it may seem and the best way to learn how to do this is by practicing. Guitar strings are fairly inexpensive and you may have to go through a few to get it right the first time you try to restring your guitar. How often you change your strings depends entirely on how much you play your guitar, but if the same strings have been on it for months, it's probably time for a new set.

Most strings attach at the headstock in the same way; however electric and acoustic guitars vary in the way in which the string is attached at the bridge. Before removing the old string from the guitar, examine the way it is attached to the guitar and try to duplicate that with the new string. Acoustic guitars may use removable bridge pins that fasten the end of the string to the guitar by pushing it into the bridge and securing it there. On some electric guitars, the string may need to be threaded through a hole in the back of the body.

Follow the series of photos below for a basic description of how to change a string. Before trying it yourself, read through the quick tips for beginners on the following page.

Use a string winder to loosen the string.

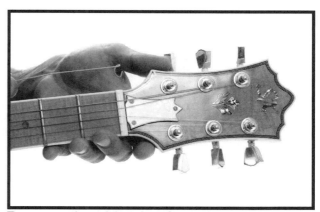

Remove the old string from the post.

Pull the string through the bridge and discard it.

Remove the new string from the packaging and uncoil it.

Thread the end of the new string through the bridge.

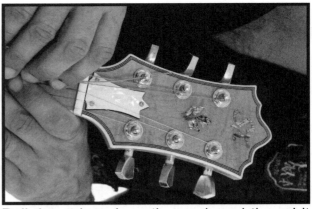
Pull the string along the neck and thread it through the small hole on the tuning post.

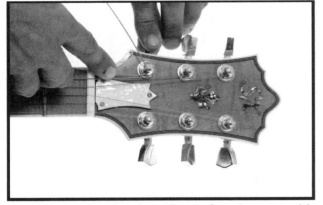
Hold the string in place just after the nut with your finger and tighten up the slack in the string with the machine head.

Carefully tighten the string and tune it to the proper pitch.

You can cut the old string off the guitar but you may want to unwind it instead and save it as a spare in case you break a string later.

Check to make sure you have the correct string in your hand before putting it on the guitar. The strings may be color coded at the end to help you identify them.

Be sure to wind the string around the tuning post in the proper direction (see photos), and leave enough slack to wind the string around the post several times. The string should wind around the post underneath itself to form a neat coil.

Once the extra slack is taken up and the string is taught, tune it very gradually to pitch, being careful not to overtighten and accidentally break the new string.

Once the string is on the guitar and tightened up, you can cut the excess string sticking out from the tuning post with a wire cutter. The sharp tail end that is left can be bent downward with the wire cutter to get it out of the way and avoid cutting or stabbing your finger. Check the ends of the string to make sure it is sitting correctly on the proper saddle and space on the nut.

New strings will go out of tune very quickly until they are broken in. You can gently massage the new string with your thumbs and fingers once it's on the guitar, slightly stretching the string out and helping to break it in. Then retune the string and repeat this process a few times for each string.

About the Author

John McCarthy
Creator of
The Rock House Method

John is the creator of The Rock House Method®, the world's leading musical instruction system. Over his 30 plus year career, he has written, produced and/or appeared in more than 100 instructional products. Millions of people around the world have learned to play music using John's easy-to-follow, accelerated programs.

John is a virtuoso musician who has worked with some of the industry's most legendary entertainers. He has the ability to break down, teach and communicate music in a manner that motivates and inspires others to achieve their dreams of playing an instrument.

As a musician and songwriter, John blends together a unique style of rock, metal, funk and blues in a collage of melodic compositions. Throughout his career, John has recorded and performed with renowned musicians including Doug Wimbish (Joe Satriani, Living Colour, The Rolling Stones, Madonna, Annie Lennox), Grammy Winner Leo Nocentelli, Rock & Roll Hall of Fame inductees Bernie Worrell and Jerome "Big Foot" Brailey, Freekbass, Gary Hoey, Bobby Kimball, David Ellefson (founding member of seven time Grammy nominee Megadeth), Will Calhoun (B.B. King, Mick Jagger and Paul Simon), Gus G of Ozzy and many more.

To get more information about John McCarthy, his music and his instructional products visit RockHouseSchool.com.

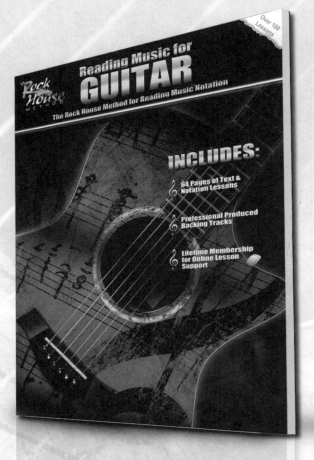